50 THRIFTY MAUI RESTAURANTS

Dining On A Budget, Island-Style

50 THRIFTY MAUI RESTAURANTS

Dining On A Budget, Island-Style

by Yvonne Biegel
and Jessica Ferracane

WATERMARK
PUBLISHING

Photography
Yvonne Biegel and Jessica Ferracane

Cover art, design, illustrations
Leo Gonzalez

Production and maps
Randall Chun Design

Library of Congress Control Number: 2003109627

ISBN 0-9742672-1-X

Watermark Publishing
1000 Bishop Street, Suite 806
Honolulu, Hawai'i 96813
Telephone: 1-808-587-7766
Toll-free 1-866-900-BOOK

e-mail: sales@bookshawaii.net
Web site: www.bookshawaii.net

Printed in the United States of America

For the two loves of my life—
Charlie and John Charles

Yvonne Biegel

To my parents, Lou and Lois,
whose exceptional cooking fueled my youth
and always ensured a clean plate

Jessica Ferracane

Contents

Foreword 1
Introduction 2

WEST SIDE 4
(Honokōwai, Kāʻanapali, Kahana,
Lahaina, Nāpili)

Breakfast
1. Castaway Cafe 6
2. Compadres Bar & Grill 8
3. Lahaina Sushiya 10
4. Moose McGillycuddy's 12
5. Soup Nutz and Java Jazz 14
6. Sunrise Cafe 16
7. Take Home Maui 18

Lunch
8. Aloha Mixed Plate 20
9. Bale French Sandwich &
   Bakery 22
10. Honokowai Okazuya & Deli 24
11. Honolua Store 26

Dinner
12. Gaby's Pizzeria & Deli 28
13. Jonny's Burger Joint 30
14. Lahaina Coolers 32
15. Penne Pasta Cafe 34
16. Thai Chef Restaurant 36

SOUTH SIDE (Kīhei, Wailea) 38

Breakfast
17. Kihei Caffe 40
18. Stella Blues Cafe 42

Lunch
19. Azeka's Ribs & Snack Shop 44
20. Da Kitchen Express 46
21. Joy's Place 48
22. Maui Tacos 50
23. Pita Paradise 52

Dinner
24. Alexander's Fish, Chicken
    and Chips 54
25. DeanO's Maui Pizza Café 56
26. Peggy Sue's 58
27. Sushi Go! 60

CENTRAL (Kahului, Wailuku)   62

Breakfast
28. Maui Coffee Roasters   64
29. Sam Sato's   66
30. Tasty Crust   68
31. The Dunes Restaurant   70

Lunch
32. Bentos & Banquets   72
33. Fiesta Time   74
34. Iao Cafe   76
35. Las Piñatas of Maui   78
36. Mama Ding's   80
37. Stillwell's Bakery   82
38. Wei Wei BBQ   84

Dinner
39. A Saigon Cafe   86
40. Brigit & Bernard's
   Garden Café   88
41. Dragon Dragon   90

NORTH SHORE/UPCOUNTRY   92
(Hāli'imaile, Kula, Makawao, Pā'ia)

Breakfast
42. Charley's Restaurant
   and Saloon   94

Lunch
43. Casanova   96
44. Hali'imaile General Store   98
45. Milagros   100
46. Paia Fishmarket   102
47. Pauwela Cafe and Bakery   104

Dinner
48. Jacques North Shore   106

EAST MAUI (Hāna, Nāhiku)   108

Lunch
49. Tutu's   110
50. Up in Smoke   112

Sweet Endings   114
Glossary   116
About the Authors   118
Index   119

Acknowledgments

Mahalo to all the wonderful local folks who responded to our surveys and gave us their invaluable input on Maui's budget dining scene. Thanks also to George Engebretson of Watermark Publishing for his support and to Pikake Kamahele, head concierge at the Four Seasons Resort Maui at Wailea, for being the very first to agree that this book was a good idea. And a special thank-you to Maui's restaurateurs—for their kind cooperation in helping create *50 Thrifty Maui Restaurants*, and for serving up all those great grinds, day after day after day!

Foreword

by Carla Tracy

When I first heard about this handy little pocket guide, my reaction was, "Now, why didn't I think of that?" In over 16 years of writing about restaurants for *The Maui News*, I am often asked where to get a really good meal at a reasonable price. It's as though the question is *déjà vu* dished up on a plate day after day.

After all, most visitors come to Maui to hang loose, relax and enjoy our island playground in casual style, no matter what their budget. I mean, let's get real—do you really want to sit through a ponderous, calorie-laden, fine-dining meal night after night when you can venture off the beaten track, wear shorts and rubber slippers (sand and all), and dine on authentic Maui offerings like a true local?

So it is with great enthusiasm that I recommend *50 Thrifty Maui Restaurants* by my esteemed journalism peers Yvonne Biegel and Jessica Ferracane. Now, instead of having to write down hard-to-find restaurants and their locations on bar napkins for inquiring visitors, I can simply say, head straight to the bookstore and buy *50 Thrifty Maui Restaurants*. It contains all the information you need.

Follow Yvonne and Jessica as they steer away from the posh resorts to Maui's hole-in-the walls (some without phones), serving everything from steaming bowls of Hawai'i's own saimin—that could cure any hangover—to Korean kal bi short ribs with a side of kim chee —so fiery hot your mouth will water—to sugar-coated, deep-fried Portuguese donuts called malassadas that a child of any age would love. You'll find that Maui's ethnic mixing bowl of restaurants is pure epicurean pleasure.

So eat, drink and be Maui, the way residents of Maui do. You—and your pocketbook—will be glad you did.

Introduction

Having worked in and around Hawai'i's hospitality industry for nearly two decades, we've seen restaurants come and go—many great concepts that just can't find a toehold in the competitive dining scene, and some not-so-great ideas that didn't even make it a month past opening.

As self-proclaimed foodies, we admit it takes something special to gain our interest. We've traveled the globe, savoring culinary masterpieces along the way and dining at the tables of some of the country's most accomplished chefs. We've also been known to scarf Vienna sausages from the can and slurp raw 'a'ama crab straight from the shell. Food-wise, we've been around, and many of the best meals we've had have been right here on our own island.

Maui is a beautiful and enticing place, attracting more than a million visitors to its shores each year. And those visitors need to eat. Many may choose to sample the posh restaurants with celebrity chefs and undeniably fabulous food.

But we hear you again and again. You want to know where the locals eat. And locals want to know where the locals eat. A Lahaina resident might not know where to eat in Kula, and vice versa. You want to slip in the door, undetected as a tourist or an out-of-towner, and order the plate lunch special or the Spam musubi with confidence. So we've done all the work for you. We've surveyed our friends, our friends' friends, cousins, aunties and even the former mayor about their favorite Maui eateries and served up the results in a menu of three-meal-a-day categories, divided by the island's geography.

Take note: There are only two national chain restaurants on our list. (Can you guess which two?) The other 48 are locally owned and operated businesses. Many restaurants in this book don't have an advertising budget at all, so their clientele is built solely on word-of-mouth recommendations. Some of these places have been in business for decades, so the word must be good.

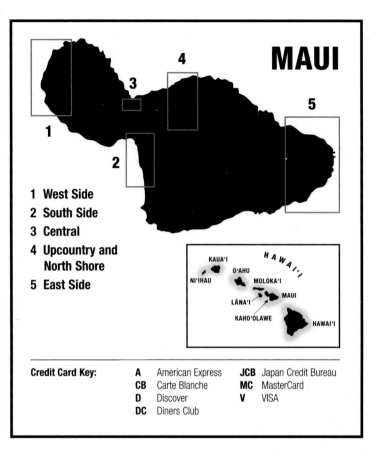

1 **West Side**
2 **South Side**
3 **Central**
4 **Upcountry and
   North Shore**
5 **East Side**

Credit Card Key:

A	American Express	**JCB**	Japan Credit Bureau
CB	Carte Blanche	**MC**	MasterCard
D	Discover	**V**	VISA
DC	Diners Club		

The breakfast and lunch items are below $10 each, and dinner entrées are under $20. All establishments must have been in operation at least one year at time of printing. Menus and prices were accurate at press time and are subject to change.

We welcome your "feed" back for future editions. Write to us c/o Watermark Publishing, 1000 Bishop Street, Suite. 806, Honolulu, Hawaii 96813.

Good grinds!
Yvonne Biegel and Jessica Ferracane

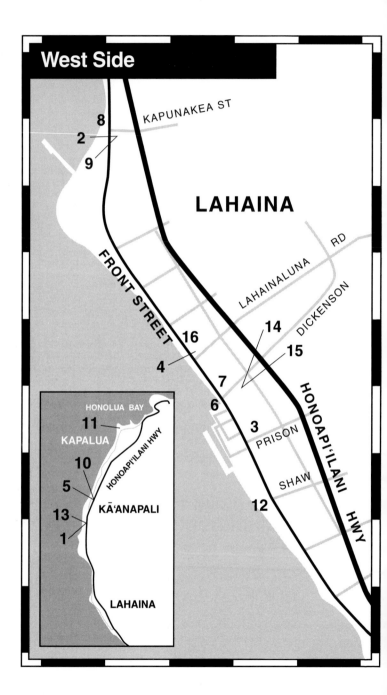

West Side

LAHAINA

KAPUNAKEA ST

FRONT STREET

LAHAINALUNA RD

DICKENSON

HONOAPI'ILANI HWY

PRISON

SHAW

8
2
9
16
4
7
6
14
15
3
12

HONOLUA BAY
11
KAPALUA
HONOAPI'ILANI HWY
10
5
KĀ'ANAPALI
13
1
LAHAINA

West Maui Restaurants
(Honōkowai, Kā'anapali, Kahana, Lahaina, Nāpili)

Breakfast
1. Castaway Cafe
2. Compadres Bar & Grill
3. Lahaina Sushiya
4. Moose McGillycuddy's
5. Soup Nutz and Java Jazz
6. Sunrise Cafe
7. Take Home Maui

Lunch
8. Aloha Mixed Plate
9. Bale French Sandwich & Bakery
10. Honokowai Okazuya Deli
11. Honolua Store

Dinner
12. Gaby's Pizzeria & Deli
13. Jonny's Burger Joint
14. Lahaina Coolers
15. Penne Pasta Cafe
16. Thai Chef Restaurant

CUISINE	**Casual American and local-style**
LOCATION	**Beachfront at Maui Kaanapali Villas; in front of the pool**
HOURS	**Daily, 7:30 a.m. to 9 p.m.; bar open until 9:30 p.m.**
SEATING	**54 inside, 30 outside**
PARKING	**Limited marked restaurant stalls; or park at Kahekili Beach Park and walk south along the paved beach walkway to the beach activities hut adjacent to Castaway Cafe**
OPENED	**1994**
ALCOHOL	**Full bar, plus a stellar wine list**
PLASTIC	**A, D, MC, V**
NOTES	**Oceanfront and poolside views**

Castaway Cafe
Maui Kaanapali Villas, 45 Kai Ala Dr., Lahaina
Telephone 661-9091

There's nothing like waking up on Maui and having a nice breakfast right next to the ocean, especially if humpback whales are splashing around offshore.

We scoped out Castaway Cafe in the middle of whale season, which is roughly from December until May. Just like at a lū'au, our food arrived before the exciting show started off the beach. We dug into a delicious, fluffy, three-egg Kaanapali Omelet ($8.50) stuffed with diced ham, mushrooms, tomatoes and Swiss cheese and topped with hollandaise. Our date, veteran whale watch captain Steve Turner, ordered Da Kine, your basic two-eggs-any-style, with rice and toast ($6.50). The coffee flowed, the eggs were perfectly cooked, and the server was as pleasant as she was quick—skills much appreciated in the morning.

Just as we finished, a pod of rambunctious humpback whales swam in fairly close to shore. It was a group of males, according to Capt. Steve, in hot pursuit of a female ahead of them. The whales leaped out of the calm morning water, pummeling each other with tails and fins in competition for the female, who soon led her pack of splashing suitors into deeper water. What a sight! Even Steve got excited, and he's seen it all.

We came in on another night for dinner, and were amazed by the wine list. Owner Gary Bush admits that his collection approaches 5,000 bottles. No wonder his wine list has won *Wine Spectator*'s Award of Excellence for the past six years.

CUISINE	**Mexican-American**
LOCATION	**Lahaina Cannery Mall**
HOURS	**Daily, 8 a.m. to 10 p.m.; bar open until 2 a.m. some nights; breakfast 8 a.m. to noon**
SEATING	**100 inside, 37 outside**
PARKING	**Plenty of free parking at the mall**
OPENED	**1991**
ALCOHOL	**Full bar**
PLASTIC	**A, D, DC, JCB, MC, V**
NOTES	**Kids eat free with paying adult on Sundays.**

Compadres Bar & Grill
Lahaina Cannery Mall, 1221 Honoapi'ilani Hwy., Lahaina
Telephone 661-7189

I f you're like us, Mexican-style food is muy bueno at any time of day—particularly for breakfast. There's something about eggs with fiery bits of jalapeno, cheese, tortillas and salsa that make getting out of bed less traumatic.

The home of the $6 breakfast, Compadres Bar & Grill may also be the only place on Maui where you can find a somewhat authentic Mexican breakfast. Sure, the menu has tried-and-true Huevos Rancheros ($6), but we were searching for something different, something Pancho Villa might cook up over a campfire in the Sierra Madres. We called our Mexican friend Jose for backup.

The Chilaquiles and Eggs ($6) caught our eye. Jose assured us that chilaquiles, which are corn tortilla chips sautéed with garlic and a potent sauce of onions and pasilla and guajillo chilies, are a Mexican tradition. At Compadres, chilaquiles are served in a skillet, topped with cotija cheese, guacamole, sour cream and two fried eggs. One bite of the massive portion and mmm…forget the Huevos Rancheros, it's chilaquiles from now on!

Jose ordered something that had his name all over it: Jose's Special, a one-egg scramble of spicy ground beef, fresh spinach, mushrooms and a side of sautéed potatoes for $6. We washed down breakfast with endless cups of coffee, but there are eye-openers like Bloody Marys, mimosas and Tequila Marys, too.

Maui locals love Taco Tuesday. Tacos are a buck, margaritas and Coronas are $2.50, and other weekly specials make Compadres one of the best values on the island.

CUISINE	**Local-style plate lunch**
LOCATION	**Half-block from Front Street, near Dan's Greenhouse**
HOURS	**Monday–Friday, 6 a.m. to 4 p.m.**
SEATING	**20**
PARKING	**Free lot across the street, adjacent to hospital**
OPENED	**1965**
ALCOHOL	**No**
PLASTIC	**Cash only**
NOTES	**Tempura is the house specialty.**

Lahaina Sushiya
117 Prison St., Lahaina
Telephone 661-5679

Sushiya is so far off the beaten path, it's not even listed in the phone book. No need. Hungry locals have kept this tiny plate lunch establishment open since 1965.

Sushiya specializes in local-style, multi-ethnic "comfort" food: kālua pork and cabbage, tempura, macaroni salad, beef curry stew, cone sushi and Spam, fondly dubbed "the Hawaiian steak." Not just plain Spam, mind you. Tempura batter-fried Spam is a mere 75 cents a slice.

We had to try it. The tempura batter was excellent, but swallowing Spam at 7 a.m. is like choking down a tequila worm, except it's bigger and really salty. We asked for a coffee chaser.

"Coffee no go with this kine food," explained owner Ok-Cha Ito.

We split a can of Coke instead, as well as the homemade kim chee, a crunchy, spicy Korean pickled cabbage medley for 75 cents.

Next came a tasty purple slice of tempura-fried Moloka'i sweet potato, again only 75 cents. We tried a jumbo tempura shrimp ($1.95), tempura eggplant (75 cents) and just a smidgen of 'ono (delicious) kālua pork and cabbage ($5.25 a plate, with macaroni salad and rice). It was the least healthy but most eclectic breakfast we've ever eaten; so wrong, it's right.

The Moloka'i ferry crew arrived as we finished. All three of them ordered the beef curry stew plate ($4.95, with rice). It was 8 a.m. "Breakfast of champions!" one exclaimed.

CUISINE	**Casual American**
LOCATION	**Across the street from Kimo's, 2nd floor**
HOURS	**Daily, 7:30 a.m. to 2 a.m. (food served until 10 p.m.); breakfast 7:30 to 11 a.m.**
SEATING	**280**
PARKING	**Pay parking lot behind Moose's; free but limited parking nearby at Lahaina Center**
OPENED	**February 1983**
ALCOHOL	**Full bar**
PLASTIC	**A, D, DC, JCB, MC, V**
NOTES	**Unbeatable daily happy hour 3 to 6 p.m.; $2 tropical drinks and more; $1 Bud and Bud Light drafts; $3 mai tais all day; very affordable children's menus**

Moose McGillycuddy's
884 Front St., Lahaina
Telephone 667-7758

We know Moose's is *the* Lahaina hot spot for dancing and debauchery (we were once young and hip), but it's also one of the least expensive places on Maui to get loads of good food for a very reasonable price.

Take Moose's breakfast menu. Where else can you find a full order of Eggs Benedict for only $7.95, with a side of fresh fruit and a choice of potatoes, white or fried rice? Nowhere, believe us. Even cheaper is the early bird breakfast. For a mere $1.99, you get two eggs any style, two strips of bacon plus a choice of starch—as long as you go between 7:30 and 8:30 a.m.

Make sure to read down the list of Moose's Famous Omelets, made with four eggs and served with potatoes, fruit and toast (or a muffin) for only $6.95. Indulge in too many 22-ounce Bloody Marys ($3.75) and you might wolf down the Lassie Omelet, made with Kal Kan and liver snaps and served outside in a bowl. The menu has several goofy selections just to make sure you're awake.

Lunch and dinner are also fantastic bargains, with nightly early bird specials from 4 to 7 p.m. featuring $10.95 prime rib dinners, fresh locally caught fish and much more. Call in advance and ask about dollar drink nights and other special happenings at Moose's.

CUISINE	**Gourmet Bistro**
LOCATION	**Honokowai Market Place**
HOURS	**Monday–Saturday, 6 a.m. to 9 p.m.; Sunday, 6 a.m. to 5 p.m.**
SEATING	**55**
PARKING	**Plenty at Honokowai Market Place**
OPENED	**Java Jazz: November 1999 Soup Nutz: February 2001**
ALCOHOL	**Full bar**
PLASTIC	**MC, V**

Soup Nutz and Java Jazz
3350 L. Honoapiʻilani Rd., Honokōwai
Telephone 667-0787

Soup Nutz and Java Jazz is a great choice for any meal, but the fact that breakfast is served day and night got us excited.

At 8 p.m., we ordered a frittata (an open-faced omelet) laden with Italian sausage, tomato, onion, mushrooms, spinach, bell peppers and feta cheese *just because we could*. A tad pricey at $9.95, but the portion was large. I came with toast and was delicious to the last bite. Instead of having coffee, we discovered eggs and fine chardonnay were made for each other.

We just had to order dinner —in this case a juicy chicken piccata for $17.95. For dessert, we shared the best pancake on the West Side ($2.50 for one mammoth flapjack) and, *because we could*, Bombay martinis.

Java Jazz is reminiscent of the chic bistros found in San Francisco and other hip locales. It has high ceilings, a copper bar top, a tremendous sound system and fun, stylish decor. Co-owner Farzad Azad reminds us of a Persian version of Rhett Butler with his charming ways. He's also a talented artist and musician. His slightly erotic artwork (much of it of his gorgeous wife and partner Kathryn) adorns the walls, and he plays guitar for patrons several nights a week.

In our opinion, Java Jazz brews the best coffee on the West Side. Everyone from local cops and surfers to visitors and plain old worker bees have turned Java Jazz into a trendy local hangout.

CUISINE	**Gourmet deli with hot entrees and soups available**
LOCATION	**Next to the Lahaina Library on Market Street**
HOURS	**Daily, 6 a.m. to 6 p.m.; main kitchen closes at 4 p.m.**
SEATING	**50**
PARKING	**Lot across the street behind the Baldwin Home Museum**
OPENED	**June 1994**
ALCOHOL	**No**
PLASTIC	**Cash and travelers checks only**
NOTES	**Take-out available; call in order by 3 p.m. on previous day**

Sunrise Cafe
693 Front St., Lahaina
Telephone 661-8558

Sunrise Cafe in Lahaina is a charming place to start the day, and its tiny street-side deck, built around a big kukui nut tree, makes a shady perch for people watching.

The colossal cinnamon rolls ($2.75) are big enough for two to share. Pancake lovers will go ga-ga for the Chocolate Buttermilk Pancakes (or waffles, $7.95), topped with shredded dark and white chocolate, strawberries, whipped cream and, if so desired, chocolate mint syrup. Like a jolt with your morning sugar? The coffee is sublime and served piping hot.

Stay for breakfast and try one of the croissant sandwiches ($3.95) or the Sunrise Platter ($6.95). It's two scrambled eggs, choice of Portuguese sausage or bacon, fresh fruit and island-made nine-grain toast.

If breakfast isn't your bag, the lunch menu is available in the morning as well. The juicy Mango BBQ Beef Sandwich is served on a sub roll with home-made barbecue sauce and a choice of starch and veggies for $7.95. There's also a good selection of salads ($4.50 to $8.95), a Santa Fe Burrito ($9.95), home-made soup ($3.95) and many other worthwhile choices.

Sunrise Cafe is snuggled between Lahaina Harbor and Front Street, alongside a steady stream of surfers, cruise ship and charter boat passengers, delivery drivers and Front Street shopkeepers.

CUISINE	**Delicatessen**
LOCATION	**Two doors up from Front Street**
HOURS	**Daily, 6:30 a.m. to 5:30 p.m.**
SEATING	**15 on the lanai**
PARKING	**Free parking along Dickenson Street; pay lot across from Take Home Maui, behind the Baldwin Home Museum**
OPENED	**June 1986**
ALCOHOL	**No**
PLASTIC	**A, DC, MC, V**

Take Home Maui
121 Dickenson St., Lahaina
Telephone 667-7056

Take Home Maui is a funky plantation-style "house" right in the heart of Lahaina where they serve up bagels and cream cheese, tasty sandwiches, pasta salads and, if your timing's right, a great slice of coconut cake.

Lahaina locals stop here to grab a cup of coffee—still only a buck—on their way to work and to check the surf across the street. It's by far the least expensive java in town. Sit outside on the lanai and listen in on the town's gossip. There's always something going on in Lahaina.

The fresh bagels ($2.50 with cream cheese, add 30 cents each for tomato and onion) and sandwiches ($4.80 to $5.95) are delicious, and it seems everything gets an eclectic garnish of pepperoncini peppers, black olives and a slice of Maui pineapple.

We adore the veggie sandwich with provolone on a crusty French roll. There are also fresh salads, smoothies, breakfast pastries, drinks and more, all at reasonable prices.

Take Home Maui also sends Maui pineapples and other local gifts and goodies back home for vacationers via Federal Express.

Almost everyone who runs Take Home Maui, from the owner to the managers and counter help, went to school together at Lahainaluna High School up the hill. Make sure you say aloha to Kehau, the African gray parrot who guards the front. Kehau meows, whistles at good-looking women and can perfectly mimic the sounds of the bustling little street.

CUISINE	**Hawaiian and multi-ethnic plate lunches, including casual American**
LOCATION	**Oceanside, across from Cannery Mall; next to Old Lahaina Lūʻau**
WEB	**www.alohamixedplate.com**
HOURS	**Daily, 10:30 a.m. to 10 p.m.**
SEATING	**146**
PARKING	**Ample parking at restaurant and more across the street at Cannery Mall**
OPENED	**February 1997**
ALCOHOL	**Full bar**
PLASTIC	**M, V**
NOTES	**Daily happy hour 2 to 6 p.m.; $2.50 mai tais, $1.50 Bud/Bud Light; great sunsets**

Aloha Mixed Plate
1285 Front St., Lahaina
Telephone 661-3322

Aloha Mixed Plate gets our vote as the best place on Maui to experience a plate lunch and authentic Hawaiian cuisine like poi and kā'lua pig. On Maui, food with a view usually comes at a high price, but not here.

This charming outdoor restaurant is located on the ocean side of Front Street, but it seems worlds away from the hubbub of downtown Lahaina. The view is an eyeful: the island of Lāna'i looms large across the denim-blue channel and dozens of sailboats are moored just offshore. You might even spot humpback whales from December through May.

The Hawaiian Plate ($7.95) is a massive serving of oh-so-moist kā'lua pig (baked to perfection in an underground oven called an imu); cooked cabbage; small sides of lomilomi salmon (salted, shredded salmon mixed with tomatoes and onions) and that quintessential Hawaiian staple, poi; plus macaroni salad and rice, two essential ingredients in a local-style plate lunch.

The mixed plate lunch was born in the early days of Hawai'i's sugar industry, when multi-ethnic workers gathered at lunchtime and shared their cultures' foods with each other.

Go to Aloha Mixed Plate with several others so you can try a little bit of everything, just like the old-time sugar cane workers. The Coconut Prawns and Chinese Roasted Duck are also excellent.

At sunset, the sun disappears behind Lāna'i just as the drums start beating at the award-winning Old Lahaina Lū'au next door. Unforgettable!

CUISINE	**Vietnamese with a French twist**
LOCATION	**Lahaina Cannery Mall (also in Kahului)**
HOURS	**Daily, 10 a.m. to 9 p.m.**
SEATING	**70-plus**
PARKING	**Plenty of free parking at the mall**
OPENED	**May 2000**
ALCOHOL	**No**
PLASTIC	**MC, JCB, V**

Bale French Sandwich & Bakery
Lahaina Cannery Mall, 1221 Honoapiʻilani Hwy., Lahaina
Telephone 661-5566

Who would have known that a shopping mall food court would dish up some of the best, most reasonably priced food on Maui? Certainly not us, so we were pleasantly surprised by Bale *(bah-lay)* French Sandwich & Bakery at Lahaina Cannery Mall.

For $3.50, you can walk away with a massive, extraordinary meal like the popular lemongrass chicken sandwich. This mouthwatering feast is a lemongrass chicken curry served in supremely crusty, freshly baked French bread and dressed up with pickled daikon radish, carrot, onion, parsley, cucumber and homemade mayonnaise. It's the most original sandwich we've tasted in years, so we kept ordering.

Next was Bale's pork sandwich (also $3.50), which is kind of like getting a plate lunch in a bun; then came a pair of fresh and healthy vegetarian tofu rolls ($4.50) served in rice wrappers with a peanut dipping sauce.

Bale also serves a variety of Vietnamese soups called "pho" for $6.25 to $6.50. The soups are rich but clear and are served with bean sprouts, basil, chili pepper and lemon. Try the chicken pho for a Southeast Asian version of the classic American cure-all, chicken noodle soup.

Owner Mike Nguyen left Vietnam for America in 1978 and came to Maui in 1985. He recently bought Bale's popular Lahaina franchise, and is one of the hardest working men we know. But he's always smiling and is proud of his fantastic little mall restaurant.

So are we.

CUISINE	**Multi-ethnic**
LOCATION	**AAAAA Rent-A-Space Mall**
HOURS	**Monday–Saturday: lunch, 10 a.m. to 2:30 p.m.; dinner, 4:30 p.m. to 9 p.m.; closed Sundays and major holidays**
SEATING	**8 inside, 8 outside**
PARKING	**Free parking lot in front**
OPENED	**November 1997**
ALCOHOL	**No**
PLASTIC	**Cash only**
NOTES	**Bring a picnic blanket. Honokōwai Beach Park down the street is a nice place to eat dinner and watch the sunset.**

Honokowai Okazuya & Deli
3600 L. Honoapi'ilani Rd., Lahaina
Telephone 665-0512

This little hole-in-the wall has to be the most popular take-out joint in West Maui. Honokowai Okazuya made nearly every single survey we got back, so it's no wonder they're sometimes too busy to take phone orders. If the phone rings and rings, it might be a Sunday (they're closed) or it could be rush hour. Just head down and order at the counter like everyone else.

"Our record was over 600 plates one day. We make one-and-a-half meals a minute," says partner/chef John McKivor.

What's impressive is that the food is always fantastic—and there's lots of it. The most popular item is Mahimahi Lemon Caper ($9.45). We lust for the spicy Kung Pao Chicken and the barbecued Korean-Style Chicken, both $6.45. The juicy six-ounce Teriyaki Steak ($7.45) is luscious, too. It's easy to play the field when there are so many eligible choices on the menu. Meals come with rice and either macaroni salad or stir-fried vegetables, or both for 95 cents extra.

The deli sandwiches, burgers, veggie selections, pasta dishes and rice bowls are also reportedly delicious, but we've always stuck to the local-style items above. But it's good to know that there's something for everyone on the menu.

The owners are veterans of Maui's hotel/restaurant industry, bringing with them decades of experience and talent that have made their restaurant a West Side treasure.

Okazuya is Japanese for "little side-dish shop," but in Hawai'i it means a local-style deli.

CUISINE	**Local-style/American**
LOCATION	**Near The Ritz-Carlton, Kapalua and the Kapalua Bay Golf Course**
HOURS	**Breakfast served daily from 6 a.m. to 10 a.m.; lunch daily from 10 a.m. to 3 p.m.; store closes at 8 p.m.**
SEATING	**24 at outside picnic tables**
PARKING	**Free parking stalls**
OPENED	**Food service began in 1976 with the Kapalua Bay Golf Course's debut**
ALCOHOL	**No**
PLASTIC	**Beer, wine and spirits available for purchase, but no drinking on premises**
NOTES	**A, D, DC, JCB MC, V**

Honolua Store
502 Office Rd., Kapalua
Telephone 669-6128

Honolua Store has been open for decades as a general store for pineapple plantation workers, but it didn't start serving ready-to-eat food until the Kapalua Bay Course was completed in 1976.

Now locals, surfers, golfers and guests of Kapalua's super-posh resorts drop by for quick, casual breakfasts and lunches at non-resort prices.

On the breakfast menu are predictable basics like bagels with cream cheese ($1.50 each); bacon (five strips for $1.75); big belly pleasers like the Loco Moco (a grilled hamburger patty topped with an egg and gravy, $3.95); and biscuits and gravy for $3.95. There are also fresh fruits, hot coffee and many types of beverages.

For lunch, there's a made-to-order deli sandwich for $5.25 and fried onion rings for $2.95— or you can choose to be really health-conscious and get a fresh green salad for $4.25. The daily plate lunch specials run $5.25 (roast pork on Wednesdays; kālua pig and cabbage on Fridays) and often sell out before noon.

Honolua Store doubles as a mini-mart and logo shop. You'll find everything from beer to candy, milk, Maui pineapples, guidebooks, Kapalua golf apparel and Hawaiian crafts. It's one-stop shopping in a quaint, plantation-style building, and the last stop to provision if you're headed north for a trip around West Maui.

CUISINE	**Italian and American**
LOCATION	**Streetside at 505 Front Street**
HOURS	**Daily, 11 a.m. to midnight; menu served until 10 p.m., slices till closing; happy hours noon to 3 p.m., 9:30 to 11:30 p.m.**
SEATING	**40**
PARKING	**Free parking lot on the corner of Front and Shaw Streets; paid parking underneath 505 Front Street**
OPENED	**February 2000**
ALCOHOL	**Full bar; draft beers**
PLASTIC	**MC, V**
NOTES	**Multiple "Taste of Lahaina" festival winner; happy hour offers $2 cheese pizza slices, $2 drafts, $3 well drinks**

Gaby's Pizzeria & Deli
505 Front St., Lahaina
Telephone 661-8112

Gaby's is one of those "take you by surprise" places. We dropped by for pizza, but were wowed by everything else on the menu.

Manager Chris Mahon created the extraordinary menu and most of the recipes. His Original Pizza Rolls won two categories at the 2000 Taste of Lahaina event for Best Meat Dish and Best Vegetarian Dish. The rolls are similar to calzone, but sliced like sushi. The Spicy Italian Sausage Roll ($10.95) was the meat winner, and it's no wonder. A large, high-grade Italian sausage is blanketed in fresh pizza dough and mozzarella, baked and served sliced on a bed of homemade marinara, peppers and onions. Outrageously delicious and big! Two people should share it, along with some other selections.

The vegetarian winner was Gaby's California roll ($10.95)—same concept, but rolled with pesto, feta cheese, sun-dried tomatoes, Maui onions, artichoke hearts and roasted red peppers, and served sushi-style with dipping sauces on the side.

Everything at Gaby's is homemade. Mahon even grates fresh, quality mozzarella and other cheeses by hand, instead of using the cheaper, pre-shredded cheese products most pizza places now use.

The pizza is available thin-crust or thick and doughy, Sicilian-style. We liked the thin-crust Clam & Garlic ($22 for a 14-inch pie, $2.75 a slice). Chris's Hot Philly Cheesesteak sandwich, we're told, is the best on the island, and comes with pasta salad ($8.95).

There's also a superlative steamed clams appetizer ($10.95) and many other surprises on the menu.

CUISINE	**Casual American**
LOCATION	**Below Luigi's at the entrance to the Kāʻanapali Resort**
HOURS	**Food served daily from 11:30 a.m. until midnight; bar open until 2 a.m.**
SEATING	**30**
PARKING	**Plenty available in parking lot**
OPENED	**1998**
ALCOHOL	**Full bar and draft beers**
PLASTIC	**A, D, DC, JCB, MC, V; $10 minimum purchase required**
NOTES	**Luigi's uses fresh, ripe tomatoes from the owners' tomato farm in Olowalu. What a difference!**

Jonny's Burger Joint
2291 Kā'anapali Pkwy., Kā'anapali
Telephone 661-4500

Just when we thought there was no escaping Maui's ubiquitous $12 hamburger, we stumbled into Jonny's Burger Joint in Kā'anapali. Yes, you read that right: Kā'anapali, home of the over-priced, underwhelming resort hamburger. Jonny's puts them all to shame with what might be the best burger on Maui. For $4.99, you get Jonny's Bigger Burger (actually the smallest burger on the menu), a grilled six-ounce patty served on a fresh bun (baked daily at Homemade Bakery in Wailuku) with pickle slabs, home-grown tomato, lettuce, special sauce and, if you like, onions. The juicy burger is hand-formed and therefore not perfectly round, and hangs out beyond the bun like it's supposed to.

Like fried onion rings? Jonny's are crispy and cost just $3.49 for a generous side order. The fries ($1.99) are great, too. There are old-fashioned milkshakes ($4.99), salads, fish sandwiches and other casual American food to try.

Jonny's has been a favorite watering hole with the local late-night crowd for years, although under different names (i.e., Burrito Brothers, Kaanapali Pizza Pub, Chicken Express). The full bar is open until 2 a.m., and it's a convenient spot for Kā'anapali restaurant and hotel workers to grab a cold one after work. Fun and games include electric dartboards, a pool table, video games and a jukebox.

CUISINE	**Global eclectic**
LOCATION	**Dickenson Square, a block and a half up from Front Street**
HOURS	**Daily, 8 a.m. to 2 a.m.; full menu until midnight; happy hour 3 to 6 p.m.**
SEATING	**65 plus 20 bar seats**
PARKING	**Plenty of free parking in back of Dickenson Square**
OPENED	**March 1989**
ALCOHOL	**Full bar, excellent wines, draft beers, microbrews**
PLASTIC	**A, D, DC, MC, V and ATM cards**
NOTES	**The largest marlin ever caught by a woman in Maui waters (955 pounds) is mounted near the bar.**

Lahaina Coolers Restaurant & Bar
180 Dickenson St., Lahaina
Telephone 661-7082

Lahaina Coolers serves the full menu every night until midnight, but that's just one of its many redeeming qualities.

The food is marvelous, and most ingredients come from local farmers and fishermen. Certain items, like the kālua pig tacos appetizer ($7.95) and the Evil Jungle Pasta (linguine pasta tossed with chicken breast, onions, peppers and a spicy Thai peanut sauce for $14.95) are so popular there would be a riot if they took them off the menu. But selections do change regularly, giving Chef Will Munder a chance to strut his culinary prowess.

We tried Munder's Crab Wontons priced at $7.50. He stuffs the crisp wontons with blue crab, papaya, shallots, cream cheese and spices, then serves them with his sweet and hot silky sauce. Yum!

Co-owner Steve Whiston told us he buys his fresh fish from local Lahaina anglers, not from ocean-depleting longliners, which relieved our companion, a Maui-based marine biologist. The nightly fish special runs about $20.

Our favorite salad is the Fried Brie on Kula Greens ($10.95). A log of Brie cheese is blanketed in a lumpia wrapper, fried and served on greens with pine nuts, poached pears and passion fruit vinaigrette. We ate the rest for breakfast; it was *that* good.

About 70 percent of Coolers' customers are locals, and most of those are regulars. Many of them consider Coolers "the 'Cheers' of the Pacific."

CUISINE	**Mediterranean/Italian**
LOCATION	**2 blocks up from Front Street at Dickenson Square**
HOURS	**Monday–Thursday, 11 a.m. to 9:30 p.m.; Friday, 11 a.m. to 10 p.m.; Saturday, 5 p.m. to 10 p.m. (closed for lunch); Sunday, 5 p.m. to 9 p.m. (closed for lunch)**
SEATING	**24 inside, 10 outside**
PARKING	**Free parking lot at Dickenson Square, also parking on Dickenson Street**
OPENED	**February 2001**
ALCOHOL	**Beer and wine available**
PLASTIC	**A, JCB, MC, V**

Penne Pasta Cafe
180 Dickenson St., Lahaina
Telephone 661-6633

This quaint neighborhood nook serves some of the best Italian and Mediterranean food on Maui—and there's nothing on the menu over $9.95.

Ten bucks buys a huge bowl of steaming spaghetti in pomodoro (tomato) sauce, loaded with baby calamari and generously seasoned with garlic and peppers. For $5.95, try the crisp, flatbread pizza topped with Greek olives, capers, basil, oregano and roasted peppers.

The last time we were there, Chef Mark Ellman wooed us with his daily veggie special. He roasted half a butternut squash with garlic and butter, then anointed the center with slivered almonds and fresh sage. Mind-bendingly delicious! This is a must-try if available.

The Bolognese Fettuccine is also a must ($7.95), and there are excellent salads big enough to share, including an 'ahi tuna Niçoise ($9.95).

Wine is never more than $5.50 a glass and there's always something worthy. Beer, soft drinks and sparkling Pellegrino water are also available.

At Penne Pasta Cafe, you get take-out prices in a sit-down restaurant, complete with table coverings from the south of France. Order at the counter (there are no servers per se; the manager brings your food to you) and share a little of this, a little of that, family style. Top off dinner with a classic tiramisu dessert ($5.95).

Perfecto!

CUISINE	**Thai**
LOCATION	**Old Lahaina Center**
HOURS	**Lunch: Monday–Friday, 11 a.m. to 2 p.m.; dinner nightly, 5 p.m. until closing (around 9:30 p.m.)**
SEATING	**20**
PARKING	**Free parking at Old Lahaina Center**
OPENED	**1984**
ALCOHOL	**BYOB**
PLASTIC	**D, DC, JCB, MC, V**
NOTES	**Excellent vegetarian choices**

16

Thai Chef Restaurant
880 Front St., Lahaina
Telephone 667-2814

Thai Chef has won all kinds of newspaper and magazine awards for its tremendously flavorful, authentic cuisine. It's also BYOB, which appeals to the thrifty-minded. Thus we arrived armed with our own lager when we dropped by for a stealthy review.

There are 61 items on the menu, and another 19 vegetarian items to choose from, so making up your mind can be quite a feat. Somehow we zeroed in on the Pad Pet, a sautéed meat dish that's very popular in Thailand.

We were elated with the choice. Pad pet ($9.85) is a spicy (if you want it to be) stir-fry of chicken, beef or pork with black mushrooms, onions, red and green bell peppers, bamboo shoots, baby corn, carrots, fresh basil and homegrown kaffir lime leaves. We ordered ours medium hot, with chicken and a side of rice.

We plunged our chopsticks right in. Soon lips and taste buds tingled with the fiery spices, and a fine sheen of sweat glazed our foreheads. We were blissed out from the hot, exotic flavors. It's hard to believe such a flavorful dish is prepared without butter or oil.

A velvety scoop of homemade Thai coconut ice cream ($3.25) puts out the fire in the mouth, but the desire to go back for more burns much longer.

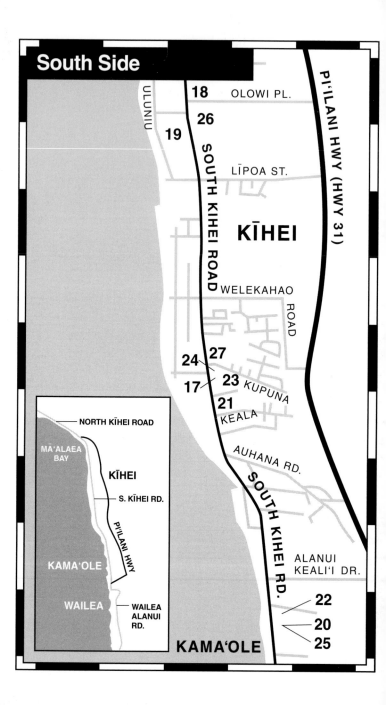

South Side

OLOWI PL.
18
26
19
LĪPOA ST.
ULUNIU
SOUTH KIHEI ROAD
PI'ILANI HWY (HWY 31)
KĪHEI
WELEKAHAO ROAD
24 27
17 23 KUPUNA
21 KEALA
AUHANA RD.
SOUTH KIHEI RD.
ALANUI KEALI'I DR.
22
20
25
KAMA'OLE

NORTH KĪHEI ROAD
MĀ'ALAEA BAY
KĪHEI
S. KĪHEI RD.
PI'ILANI HWY
KAMA'OLE
WAILEA
WAILEA ALANUI RD.

South Side Restaurants
(Kīhei, Wailea)

Breakfast
17. Kihei Caffe
18. Stella Blues Cafe

Lunch
19. Azeka's Ribs & Snack Shop
20. Da Kitchen Express
21. Joy's Place
22. Maui Tacos
23. Pita Paradise

Dinner
24. Alexander's Fish, Chicken & Chips
25. DeanO's Maui Pizza Café
26. Peggy Sue's
27. Sushi Go!

CUISINE	**Fresh baked goods and gourmet sandwiches**
LOCATION	**Next to Union 76**
HOURS	**Monday–Friday, 5 a.m. to 8:30 p.m.; Saturday and Sunday, 5 a.m. to 3 p.m.**
SEATING	**86**
PARKING	**Free parking across the street**
OPENED	**1992**
ALCOHOL	**No**
PLASTIC	**Cash or travelers checks only**
NOTES	**Will make picnic baskets with advance notice**

17

Kihei Caffe
1215 S. Kīhei Rd. #512, Kīhei
Telephone 874-3779

This is probably as close as Maui gets to a Parisian outdoor café.

Alfresco tables under a canopied lanai are filled with an eclectic mix of locals chatting about the previous night's escapades and jet-lagged visitors adjusting to a new time zone. The intimate restaurant along South Kīhei Road is a leisurely two-mile walk from most Wailea resorts and within easy reach from the many Kīhei condos.

Open at 5 a.m. daily, Kihei Caffe serves up cups of Maui Oma Coffee for $1.50—Kona Gourmet and flavored roasts. The pastries are made in-house daily and range in price from $1.25 to $2.50, including cinnamon rolls and sticks, mango and coconut muffins, apple twists, cherry popovers and pound cake.

We perused the menu of familiar breakfast fare and jumped at the Breakfast Burrito: scrambled eggs with melted cheese and grilled home fries, salsa and jalapenos rolled in a large flour tortilla ($5.95). After awakening our taste buds with the spicy pepper, we tried the Southern-style Biscuits and Sausage Gravy ($4.95), a filling transition.

The real deal on the menu is the grilled steak and eggs with home fries ($8.95). You can substitute mahimahi or 'ahi for the steak for the same price.

Always a breakfast and lunch favorite, Kihei Caffe is under new ownership and now serves dinner—lucky for those who enjoy home-cooked favorites such as liver and onions and chicken fried steak.

CUISINE	**Wholesome American**
LOCATION	**Azeka II Shopping Center**
WEB	**http://www.maui.net/~stelablu/**
HOURS	**Daily, 7:30 a.m. to 9 p.m.**
SEATING	**80**
PARKING	**Free parking at Longs Center**
OPENED	**1991**
ALCOHOL	**Beer, wine and tropical drinks**
PLASTIC	**D, MC, V**

18

Stella Blues Cafe
1279 S. Kīhei Rd. (Azeka II Shopping Center), Kīhei
Telephone 874-3779

Grateful Dead fans around the world have flocked to this Deadhead cafe since its opening in 1991. Passing the memorabilia of Deadhead posters and T-shirts, we come to pay homage to the food, not Jerry Garcia.

Though Stella Blues serves only quality, grain-fed, chemical-free beef, we couldn't resist the Garden Melt, a "Made on Maui" vegetarian patty topped with Swiss cheese and grilled onions on fresh grilled caraway rye with a side of Russian dressing ($7.95). It's surprisingly flavorful.

So where's the beef, you ask? We perused the meat options and treated ourselves to the French Dip Sandwich ($8.95), moist and tender roast beef piled high on a French roll.

Also a well-known breakfast spot, Stella Blues keeps the Late Riser on the menu after 11 a.m. every day: two eggs, ham or bacon and toast ($7.95). Non-alcoholic beverages include a surprising lineup of Italian sodas, blended drinks and our favorite, Kelly's Coffee: layers of milk, espresso and chocolate over ice and topped with whipped cream ($3.50). Beer and wine are available as well as assorted tropical drinks.

Stella Blues, easily accessible on your way in or out of town, moved in June 2003 to a bigger location with a full bar and fryer (think French fries).

CUISINE	**Local-style, take-out plate lunch and ribs**
LOCATION	**Azeka Place I Makai**
HOURS	**Daily, 7:30 a.m. to 3 p.m.**
SEATING	**No inside seating; 20 seats outside**
PARKING	**Ample free parking at Azeka Place I**
OPENED	**April 1950**
ALCOHOL	**No**
PLASTIC	**A, D, MC, V and debit cards**

19

Azeka's Ribs & Snack Shop
1280 S. Kīhei Rd. (Azeka Place I), Kīhei
Telephone 879-0078

The longest running restaurant in Kīhei, Azeka's Ribs & Snack Shop was around before any of the traffic lights or fancy oceanfront homes sprouted up along South Kīhei Road.

Owned and operated by one of Kīhei's oldest families, the Azekas, the no-fuss walk-up window makes grabbing lunch on the go a breeze. You'll find the restaurant tucked into the corner of Azeka Place I shopping mall next to Ace Hardware.

This is great take-out with a list of plate lunches and rotating specials from hot dogs ($2.25) to chopped steak ($5.95) and pork tofu ($6.25). Familiar sandwiches make feeding kids easy: hearty egg salad or tuna salad ($2.50 each). A list of side orders includes saimin ($2.75) and laulau ($4.50) —pork, beef and spinach wrapped in a ti leaf and steamed to lock in the flavors.

The chow fun ($2.95), a local noodle favorite, sells out almost daily. It's a wide Chinese egg noodle dish cooked with pork, green onion and bean sprouts and seasoned, then stir fried.

But Azeka's is known around the island for its Rib Plate ($6.25). It includes three pieces of kalbi ribs, two scoops rice, mac salad and kim chee. If two of you want to split dinner, opt for a side order of ribs ($4.50 for about 16 ounces) and a tub of potato/macaroni salad for $3.15. You can also get sushi to go, including cone sushi and maki (75 cents each) and the ever-favorite local snack, Spam musubi ($1.35).

If you prefer to eat here, four shaded picnic benches are available, and the condiment table packs plenty of napkins for quick and easy clean-up. Try the homemade Hawaiian chili pepper water, the local hot sauce, and use chopsticks.

CUISINE	**Local and Hawaiian food**
LOCATION	**Rainbow Mall; also located at Triangle Square in Kahului (lunch and dinner only)**
HOURS	**Daily, 9 a.m. to 9 p.m.**
SEATING	**60**
PARKING	**Plenty of free parking at the mall**
OPENED	**1997**
ALCOHOL	**No**
PLASTIC	**Cash and travelers checks only**

20

Da Kitchen Express
2439 S. Kīhei Rd. (Rainbow Mall), Kīhei
Telephone 875-7782

We took a break from snorkeling at Kama'ole Beach Park and walked across the street in our "slippahs" and swimsuits to an unassuming eatery, Da Kitchen Express, at the back of Rainbow Mall. We joined other locals grabbing take-out or dining in for lunch.

The restaurant packs 'em in, because it packs on heaping portions of local-style food. Our favorite is the Hawaiian Plate Lunch ($8.50)—a pork laulau (pork wrapped in ti and taro leaves and steamed so the flavors seep into the meat) served with kālua (smoked) pork, chicken long rice and lomilomi salmon. It's the restaurant version of a lū'au without the hula dancers and drums.

The Teriyaki Plate is four pieces of chicken marinated in teriyaki sauce and charbroiled to seal in the flavor ($5.75). All plate lunches are served with two scoops of sticky white rice and potato macaroni salad mixed with mayonnaise, or a healthier alternative of mixed greens. You can request extra meat on your plate for $1.50 more.

The meat portions of the plate lunch are also served in sandwiches on a toasted onion bun—Teriyaki Chicken Sandwich ($5.25) or Kalua Pork Sandwich ($5.25), and Mahimahi Fish Sandwich ($5.75.) Add cheese or a side order of French fries for only $1. There are no substitutions allowed.

Even we were surprised to hear that Da Kitchen serves breakfast from 9 to 11 a.m. The Special Omelet is choice at $5.75 for a combination of tomato, mushroom, onion, cheese and Portuguese sausage, served with home fries or rice. Da best!

CUISINE	**Healthy organic**
LOCATION	**Island Surf building on the Auhana Street side**
HOURS	**Monday–Saturday, 10 a.m. to 5 p.m.**
SEATING	**8 inside; or bring lunch to Kalama Park across the street**
PARKING	**Plenty of free parking nearby**
OPENED	**January 1998**
ALCOHOL	**No**
PLASTIC	**A, MC, V**

21

Joy's Place
1993 S. Kīhei Rd., Kīhei
Telephone 879-9258

Joy doesn't advertise and she doesn't even have an answering machine, so we were lucky when a friend told us to check out what is easily the best health food on the island.

Before you meat lovers turn the page, know this: just because Joy's Place is all about healthy, organic eating doesn't mean there's no meat on the menu. *Au contraire!* Her turkey sandwich is a smash hit, featuring slices of organically raised, oven-roasted turkey with provolone cheese, ripe avocado and all the fixings—lettuce, tomato, onion, grated carrot, clover sprouts and mayo or Vegenaise—for $7.50.

But the Joy Roll is the ultimate lunchtime joy ride. It's a kind of burrito made with lettuce, fresh ginger, garlic, brown rice, avocado, grated carrot, onion, cilantro and sprouts, stuffed into a large rice wrapper lined with a sheet of mineral-rich nori (seaweed) and served with a wonderful sesame dipping sauce ($7.50). We recommend adding the locally caught tuna for a buck more. Wash it down with fresh-squeezed ginger lemonade ($2.85).

There are salads, wheat-free breads and marvelous, usually vegan, homemade soups (12 ounces for $3.95) and more. Do your body a favor and check out Joy's Place.

As Joy says, "What we eat can take away our health, or it can give it to us."

Amen.

CUISINE	**Mexican-American**
LOCATION	**Kamaʻole Beach Center (also in Napili and Kahului)**
WEB	**www.mauitacos.com**
HOURS	**Daily, 9 a.m. to 9 p.m.**
SEATING	**30**
PARKING	**Plenty of free parking at the center**
OPENED	**1995**
ALCOHOL	**No**
PLASTIC	**A, D, DC, JCB, MC, V**

22

Maui Tacos
2411 S. Kīhei Rd. (Kamaʻole Beach Center), Kīhei
Telephone 879-5005

Ready for some Mexican food with a little Mauitude? With seven locations throughout Hawaiʻi and seven on the mainland, Chef Mark Ellman mixes aloha with the right ingredients for a winning Mexican menu.

Maui Tacos is a surfer's paradise with a list of burritos named after Maui beaches and surf spots—a geography lesson in food.

No need to trek to the North Shore for the Hoʻokipa. You'll find this burrito of fresh island fish, black beans, fresh salsa, rice and sour cream rolled into an oversize flour tortilla and served with a handful of corn chips ($6.95) at Maui Tacos. And Shark Pit has moved to Kīhei disguised as a bean and cheese burrito with choice of steak or chicken ($6.25).

A la carte items include traditional enchiladas with potato ($3.50) or choice of steak or chicken ($4.99). Hard or soft tacos run from $1.99 for beans to $3.75 for fish. The fresh chips accompanying every dish are made daily in 100% cholesterol-free vegetable oil.

The complimentary salsa bar includes chopped cilantro, onions, jalapenos, quartered limes and Chef Ellman's own salsas. We like the Pineapple Passion salsa with Hawaiian pineapple, tomatillos, garlic, cilantro, sweet onion, jalapeno and lime juice. Pour it over your burrito or taco for extra punch. All the sodas run $1.59 and free refills are included.

Conveniently located across from Kīhei's three Kamaʻole beaches, Maui Tacos welcomes you in beachwear. Dine in with ample seating on simple, wood bar stools, or request take-out and get back to your favorite beach.

CUISINE	**Mediterranean with a Greek flair**
LOCATION	**Kihei Kalama Village**
HOURS	**Monday–Saturday, lunch, 11 a.m. to 5 p.m.; dinner, 5 p.m. to 9:30 p.m.; Sunday, 5 p.m to 9:30 p.m. (no lunch on Sunday)**
SEATING	**30 outside on the deck, 20 inside**
PARKING	**Plenty of free parking**
OPENED	**May 1999**
ALCOHOL	**Beer and wine**
PLASTIC	**MC, V**
NOTES	**A favorite with South Maui vegetarians**

23

Pita Paradise
1913 S. Kīhei Rd., Kīhei
Telephone 875-7679

The handmade pita bread at Pita Paradise is so good you could wrap a shoe in it and we'd consider eating it.

Maybe not a shoe, but definitely a salad. The Greek Salad Pita ($6.95) is a blend of greens, Maui onions, Greek olives, feta cheese, herbs, cucumbers and tomatoes, tossed with a yogurt dressing and tucked into a warm, thick round pita. It's a fun way to eat healthier.

The heavenly hummus is another healthy choice. Hummus is a spread made from puréed chickpeas, and here it's served with pita bread for $4.95.

For the carnivorous crowd, there are pitas and kabobs made with lamb, steak, chicken and fish. If the owner doesn't reel in the fresh fish himself, he buys it from local anglers, making a special point not to support commercial longliners. We enjoyed the grilled 'ahi tuna kabob ($13.95, with pitas, vegetables and potatoes).

Lamb fans will love the tender, lean lamb pita ($8.95). All pitas come with herbed roasted potatoes, a welcome break from the "fries or chips" choice.

Pita Paradise does a lot of take-out business, but if you have time, enjoy your meal on the shady wooden deck. Two leafy ficus trees keep the deck fully protected from the hot Kīhei sun. Come at night, when little white lights add a twinkle to the canopy.

CUISINE	**Fresh seafood, chicken, ribs and more**
LOCATION	**Kihei Kalama Village**
HOURS	**Daily, 11 a.m. to 9 p.m.**
SEATING	**80**
PARKING	**Free parking behind the restaurant and at Kihei Kalama Village**
OPENED	**July 1991**
ALCOHOL	**No**
PLASTIC	**V, MC**

24

Alexander's Fish, Chicken and Chips
1913 S. Kīhei Rd., Kīhei
Telephone 874-0788

Alexander's serves up more than fish and chips in a small shop across the street from Kalama Park, making it easy to grab an early dinner after a long day on the beach. With a counter walk-up indoors manned by a friendly staff, it's common to see the line forming all the way outside.

Well worth the wait, Alexander's is the place locals on the south side stop for quick, affordable seafood. Have it your way, as menu items are offered broiled or fried in 100% canola oil.

The popular fish and chip meals include slaw and choice of French fries or white rice. The fresh and tasty 'ahi, mahimahi or ono plates offer three filets for $7.25. We love the shrimp and calamari served in paper baskets and priced at $8.50 each, and the oysters are phenomenal for just $9.70. The tartar/cocktail sauce concoction at the condiment bar is the restaurant's original recipe, and it's great with everything.

Side orders and pūpū include hush puppies for a buck, zucchini at $3.25 and mushrooms at $4.25. We dipped all three into ranch dressing. There are combo meals and sandwiches on the varied menu, and a small garden salad is offered at $3.50. Planning a picnic? Then consider the 13-piece a la carte basket for the family (from $16.25 for chicken to $19.95 for ribs).

Be forewarned that Alexander's doesn't sell beer, which we think would complement the beer-friendly menu. But it's a great scene for people-watching on the casual lanai fronting on South Kīhei Road.

CUISINE	**Pizza and more**
LOCATION	**Upstairs in Rainbow Mall**
HOURS	**Daily, 11:30 a.m. to 10 p.m.**
SEATING	**100**
PARKING	**Ample free parking at mall**
OPENED	**October 2000**
ALCOHOL	**Full bar**
PLASTIC	**A, D, DC, JCB, MC, V**
NOTES	**Live entertainment nightly**

25

DeanO's Maui Pizza Café
2439 S. Kīhei Rd., Kīhei
Telephone 891-2200

Chef DeanO is a graduate of the Culinary Institute of America and worked in five-star kitchens before joining his family on Maui to open DeanO's Maui Pizza Café. He's created the pizza mecca of the south side, rivaling even Wolfgang Puck's for originality. The atmosphere is open and inviting, with a large bar in the center of the room providing a friendly space for dining alone or cocktails.

The pizzas are large enough to share, and the prices range from $12.50 to $16.25. We ordered Da Works for $16.25. This big combo is perfect for people who can't decide what toppings they want on a pizza. It comes with everything—sausage, bell peppers, pepperoni, mushrooms, onions, roasted garlic and cheese.

But we are in Hawai'i, so we also ordered the Local Boy.

It's a pizza topped with tender kālua (smoked) pork, sweet Maui onion, pineapple, tomato sauce and mozzarella cheese for $14.75. Loved it!

We inadvertently discovered the best-tasting buffalo wings on the planet, the Pacific Isle Sweet Chili Wings at $7.95. These tender chicken wings are deep-fried and then sautéed in a sweet chili sauce and sprinkled with fired-roasted sesame seeds. Blue cheese dipping sauce is served on the side. Fabulous!

There is also an assortment of salads and pastas including the Pesto Topaz Pasta. The pesto is made with fresh basil and other herbs that Chef DeanO hand-selects from local vendors.

There is live entertainment nightly and karaoke after 10 p.m., and a magic and comedy show Monday nights at 7 p.m. Call ahead for reservations as seating is limited.

CUISINE	**1950s diner: burgers, shakes, the works**
LOCATION	**Azeka Place II**
HOURS	**Sunday–Thursday, 11 a.m. to 9 p.m.; Friday and Saturday, 11 a.m. to 10 p.m.**
SEATING	**54**
PARKING	**Free parking at shopping center**
OPENED	**December 1993**
ALCOHOL	**No**
PLASTIC	**DC, MC, V**
NOTES	**Check out Maui's vintage hot rods on "Come Cruise Car Night," held the first Saturday of each month at 7 p.m.**

26

Peggy Sue's
1279 S. Kīhei Rd. (Azeka Place II), Kīhei
Telephone 875-8944

Whether you're old enough to reminisce about dime store soda fountains or just want to take a step back in time, Peggy Sue's harkens to the era of rock-n-roll, Hollywood glamour and flashy cars, all served up at a 1950s-style local diner.

Framed black-and-white glossies of Rock Hudson, Humphrey Bogart, Sammy Davis, Jr., James Dean, Elvis and other vintage celebs line the walls. Young, pretty local girls dressed in pink uniforms serve burgers, sandwiches and salads, just like a scene from an Elvis movie.

Slide into a booth with your sweetheart and pop a quarter into a Wall-O-Matic jukebox which cranks out tunes from the Beach Boys, Ritchie Valens, Buddy Holly, Patsy Cline and the King himself.

Rev your engines with chili fries smothered in cheese and onions for $4.95. Or try one of the six Cadillac burger meals, a full six-ounce all-beef burger charbroiled on an open flame and served with a generous helping of low-fat and low-cholesterol oven-baked French fries ($7.75 to $9.25). We had the Big Bopper, a big bacon cheeseburger topped with lettuce, tomato, onion and mayonnaise. Make it a double-meat patty for less than $2 more.

Your little ones will love the fun at the counter soda fountain with barstools that spin, giving them a whirl of fun. The keiki menu for kids 12 and under is just as much fun.

Sodas, milk shakes and floats are served up in vintage glassware. And the luscious Roselani ice cream in shakes ($4), banana splits ($6.25), sundaes ($2.75) and other treats is made on Maui.

CUISINE	**Sushi**
LOCATION	**Kukui Mall, Kihei; also located at Ka`ahumanu Shopping Center in Kahului**
WEB	**www.sushigo.com**
HOURS	**Monday–Saturday, 11 a.m. to 9 p.m.; Sunday, 11 a.m. to 8 p.m.; Monday–Friday, closed 2 to 4 p.m.**
SEATING	**30**
PARKING	**Mall parking available**
OPENED	**December 2001**
ALCOHOL	**Sake, beer, wine**
PLASTIC	**A, D, DC, JCB, MC, V**

27

Sushi Go! Restaurant
1819 South Kīhei Rd. (Kukui Mall), Kīhei
Telephone 875-8744

Sushi is notoriously expensive, so when Sushi Go! Restaurant opened its location in Kīhei, many rejoiced. With two-piece plates priced from $1.75 to $4, this is a great restaurant for beginners, as you can try many different items.

With over 40 different kinds of sushi on the menu, we selected the most popular items locals order: Tako (octopus) and tobiko (flying fish eggs), each selling for two pieces for $1.75. The tako is exactly what you'd imagine (a bit chewy), while the tobiko pops in your mouth, a surprise in every bite. Unagi (broiled fresh water eel) and maguro (raw tuna) each sell for two pieces for $2.50.

We also indulged in fancy plates of sushi: $4 for two pieces of Go! Roll (unagi over a tobiko California roll) or Caterpillar Roll (unagi with avocado).

The "fast food" presentation at Sushi Go! is very common in Japan. Menu items are paraded along a nonstop conveyer belt like the ones at Baggage Claim. Plates of food glide through the kitchen and circle around toward you. Just grab what you see without waiting for someone to bring it to you. Everything is color-coded for pricing.

On Wednesday nights, an "all-you-can-eat-sushi" buffet is offered for $22.99 per person. The pūpū menu is kid-friendly and includes grilled steak, Korean chicken wings, chicken nuggets, shrimp scampi and fresh sashimi. Prices range from $7 to $14.99.

Sushi goes great with sake or Japanese beer. A variety of both are available, as well as a few wines.

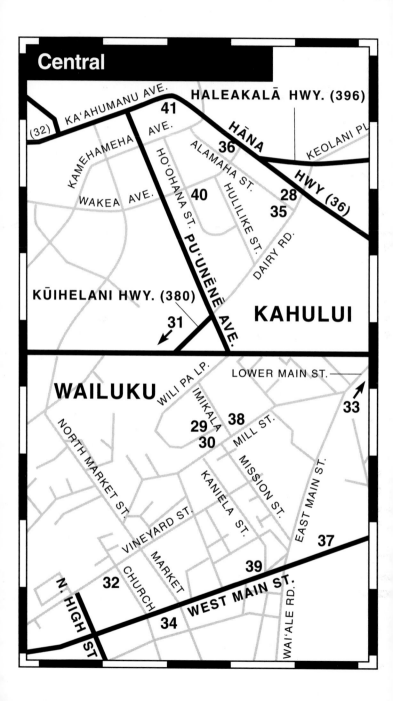

Central Restaurants
(Kahului, Wailuku)

Breakfast

28. Maui Coffee Roasters
29. Sam Sato's
30. Tasty Crust
31. The Dunes Restaurant

Lunch

32. Bentos & Banquets by Bernard
33. Fiesta Time
34. Iao Cafe
35. Las Piñatas of Maui
36. Mama Ding's Restaurant & Bakery
37. Stillwell's Bakery & Cafe
38. Wei Wei BBQ 'n Noodle House

Dinner

39. A Saigon Cafe
40. Brigit & Bernard's Garden Café
41. Dragon Dragon

CUISINE	**American/European, featuring fresh-baked items**
LOCATION	**Next to Marco's**
WEB	**www.hawaiiancoffee.com**
HOURS	**Monday–Friday, 7 a.m. to 6 p.m.; Saturday, 8 a.m. to 5 p.m.; Sunday, 8 a.m. to 2:30 p.m.**
SEATING	**50**
PARKING	**Plenty**
OPENED	**1991**
ALCOHOL	**No**
PLASTIC	**A, D, MC, V**
NOTES	**Coffee voted best on Maui by readers of *The Maui News***

28

Maui Coffee Roasters
444 Hāna Hwy., Kahului
Telephone 877-2877

Long before the big coffee chains made it to the Islands, locals voted Maui Coffee Roasters as the place serving the "Best Coffee on Maui" for the delicious java and fresh baked goods in their Kahului store.

To us, it's still one of the best coffee joints on the island. Filled with whimsical local artwork and handcrafted tables, the eatery is a venerable haven for coffee regulars looking to jump-start their day. But there's more.

Maui Coffee Roasters is known for great bagels, so we filled up on the Huevos Bagel ($4.95), scrambled eggs with the restaurant's famous green chili pesto, onions and jalapenos with melted cheddar cheese and tomatoes, served on bagel of choice. The bagel sandwiches also caught our eyes. The Crab Melt at $5.95 is a sure winner: seafood salad with melted cheddar and mozzarella cheeses, topped with tomato and sprouts.

Select your own bagel from daily varieties and coordinating spreads such as Guava Butter ($2.25) and Salmon Cream Cheese ($2.50).

Sandwiches on bread, wraps, soups and salads are popular for lunch. We like the Pilgrim Wrap for $5.95, partly for the name and mostly for the taste. The turkey, cranberries, greens and mixed veggies are drizzled with ranch dressing and stuffed into a sun-dried tomato wrap.

Espresso, cappuccino, latte—oh my! The "Best Coffee on Maui" is definitely worth a try. The company roasts its Hawaiian-grown coffee beans in its warehouse daily and bags them for sale in the store. You can buy the packaged beans to take home. Or sip the coffee of the day, such as the Pacific Coffee Blend, right inside.

Happy Cappy Hour is from 3 p.m. to closing with $1 cappuccino specials.

CUISINE	**Local**
LOCATION	**Wailuku Millyard**
HOURS	**Daily, 7 a.m. to 2 p.m.; closed Sundays**
SEATING	**50**
PARKING	**Limited free parking in front**
OPENED	**1933**
ALCOHOL	**No**
PLASTIC	**Cash only**
NOTES	**Saimin is the specialty.**

29

Sam Sato's
1750 Wili Pa Lp., Wailuku
Telephone 244-7124

One of Maui's best noodle houses, and one of our favorites, Sam Sato's was included on most of the survey sheets we received from local residents. Like many great noodle places, Sam Sato's is tucked away on a backstreet and you'll have to ask a local to find it.

The restaurant has been in business at various locations since 1933 and is currently housed in Wailuku's light industrial area, the Millyard.

Make a day of it in Central Maui with a visit to ʻĪao Valley, the Hawaiʻi Nature Center and Maui Historical Society's Bailey House Museum. Stroll Old Wailuku Town's Market Street for antiques and collectibles. Then head to Sam Sato's as any hungry local would.

We eat here so often that we didn't have to do a formal review. Take our word for it, and try the Dry Noodles, the signature dish.

It's cooked like saimin, mixed in a bowl, then drained and served with a garnish of bean sprouts, green onions and pork. A small bowl will set you back $4. If you want it Super Dry with Vegetables, that's $5.50.

These are "broke da mout'" noodles, folks. And the best remedy for a hangover that we've ever experienced.

They also serve American and local breakfast items. Plate lunches are $6 to $6.50.

The line usually extends outside where park benches provide respite for a short wait. Catch up on Maui happenings with the friendly people you'll undoubtedly meet there.

CUISINE	**Local-style diner**
LOCATION	**Outskirts of Wailuku town**
HOURS	**Daily, 5:30 a.m. to 10 p.m.**
SEATING	**115**
PARKING	**Free parking in front and back**
OPENED	**1944**
ALCOHOL	**No**
PLASTIC	**Debit cards, local checks, travelers checks and cash only**
NOTES	**The hotcakes are world famous!**

30

Tasty Crust
1770 Mill St., Wailuku
Telephone 244-0845

Tasty Crust has been around for more than 50 years, getting its name from its former incarnation as a bakery. Even former Mayor James "Kimo" Apana named this one of his favorite haunts.

The local diner's linoleum tile floors, wood-paneled walls and pegboard ceiling have weathered many a morning coffee ritual.

We always thought the name Tasty Crust came from the crusty border around the edge of its famous pancakes. A hotcake, as it's called here, is 10 inches across, fluffy and filling. It's made on a griddle lined with butter, so the edges turn crispy. One hotcake is $1.50, and the regular order of two is $3. At Tasty Crust, they serve 'em up with good old-fashioned maple syrup.

Another local favorite is the fried rice plate with an egg for $4.35. You can also get a side scoop for $1. The island's best Loco Moco is served here: a scoop of white sticky rice topped with a fried egg and hamburger patty ($3.85). The omelets ($3.25 to $4.85) are generous in size and taste, and ingredients include Spam, Portuguese sausage, Vienna sausage, shrimp and vegetables.

This is the most local diner on Maui and in true diner fashion, they serve three meals a day. The recipes are created by owner Curtis Takaoka's mother. His parents were the original owners.

You'll notice all the condiment options displayed on your table including shoyu—that's what soy sauce is called in Hawai'i. Try it on your rice and eggs.

Now this is local style!

CUISINE	**Asian-American**
LOCATION	**The Dunes at Maui Lani Golf Course**
HOURS	**Daily, 6:30 a.m. to 7:30 p.m.**
SEATING	**90, plus a banquet capacity of 250**
PARKING	**Plenty of free parking**
OPENED	**August 2001**
ALCOHOL	**Full bar**
PLASTIC	**A, MC, V**

31

The Dunes Restaurant
1333 Maui Lani Pkwy., Kahului
Telephone 877-7461

The Dunes at Maui Lani is a championship golf course designed by Nelson and Hayworth in an Old World links layout. It's a challenging course for both experienced and novice players, so it's a relief that The Dunes Restaurant's is both friendly and inviting.

Dropped between the first tee and the 18th hole, The Dunes Restaurant dining room and outdoor lanai features a breathtaking view of manicured green fairways, a small pristine pond and the rolling West Maui Mountains. The sturdy teak furniture makes for a setting so comfortable you could sit around all morning watching golfers come and go.

Weekday lunches are slammed mostly with locals who live and work close by, but it's also a great midway meeting point if you're like us—one coming from Lahaina and the other from Kīhei.

Our server was full of pep and energy. She recommended the Banana Creamed Pancake—one pancake as large as a dinner plate, swimming in a vanilla cream sauce. The plate is dusted with cinnamon and shaved macadamia nuts, making it a work of art at just $3.95.

Meat lovers will be in heaven when they taste the homemade Corned Beef Hash—made with brisket then sliced and added to diced potato, red and green bell peppers, sautéed onion and two poached eggs—and served with rice pilaf and a biscuit for $8.95.

Like the menu, rounds of golf are also affordable, starting at $95 for visitors and offering an experience that rivals that found at the big golf resorts.

CUISINE	"Local gourmet"
LOCATION	Wailuku
WEB	www.bentosandbanquets.com
HOURS	Monday–Friday, 10 a.m. to 2 p.m.; dine in or take out; delivery in Kahului/Wailuku
SEATING	20
PARKING	Along Church Street or in municipal parking lot across the street
OPENED	1991
ALCOHOL	No
PLASTIC	Cash or travelers checks only
NOTES	Catering and banquet services also available

32

Bentos & Banquets by Bernard
85 Church St., Wailuku
Telephone 244-1124

'**B**-b-b-bentos and Banquets!"

We challenge you not to paraphrase this wildly popular lunch spot to the tune of Elton John's hit "Bennie and the Jets."

Oh, but they're weird and wonderful, just like Sir Elton sings. Actually, the local-style cuisine here is hardly weird, but it is wonderful and you get plenty of it for a very fair price.

But what exactly is a bento?

Like the term "okazuya," which means "deli," bento is a Japanese word, and it refers to a lunch box divided into compartments to store small servings of food. Nowadays, the box is usually a Styrofoam container, and the dishes aren't so small, at least not at Bentos & Banquets.

Take the chicken enchilada special we sampled. For $6.25, we got two fat enchiladas with sauce, superb Spanish rice and refried beans plus a side of ultra-fresh salsa and chips. Everything is homemade, master cook (and Bernard's brother) Kawika assured us.

Order at the buffet counter, where you can scope out what you want for lunch. The Chicken Hekka Plate, perhaps? (That's sautéed chicken with a "hekka" lotta veggies, served with pork katsu, rice and potato macaroni salad, $6.25.) Or maybe the Vegetarian Tofu Delight, or any other of the healthy daily specials. A generous Caesar salad with chicken is just $7.95.

Bentos & Banquets is hidden in the heart of downtown Wailuku and caters to the local business crowd. Go during the lunch rush like we did and you might get to eavesdrop on jurors on break from the nearby courthouse. B-b-b-bentos & Banquets!

CUISINE	**Mexican**
LOCATION	**Corner of Hala Place and Lower Main Street, across from H & R Block**
HOURS	**Monday–Saturday, 11 a.m. to 9 p.m.; closed Sundays**
SEATING	**8 stools inside; more a take-out than a dine-in place**
PARKING	**A few stalls provided on the right side and in front of the building**
OPENED	**March 2000**
ALCOHOL	**No**
PLASTIC	**Cash only**
NOTES	**Niño- and niña-size meals available upon request for children**

33

Fiesta Time
1132 Lower Main St., Wailuku
Telephone 249-8463

It's a challenge to find decent, authentic Mexican food on Maui—a fact lamented by just about everyone, especially Maui's growing Hispanic population.

When we polled our Mexican friends about their favorite places to get bona fide Mexican food on Maui, only one place came up: Fiesta Time in Wailuku.

Owner Raúl Jaimes came to Hawai'i 38 years ago from Mexico City. Fiesta Time looks like Raúl had it shipped over with him. It's a small cinderblock structure painted white, with a huge, colorful mural of a "Revolucion Señorita" painted on the ocean-facing wall outside.

Inside, the south-of-the border menu is muy excellente. Don't miss the Al Pastor tacos ($6.95), spicy, mouthwatering grilled pork tacos served in soft corn tortillas with rice and beans (and made with soybean oil instead of lard). Top 'em with delicious homemade salsa, and wash 'em down with cold horchata, a chilled Mexican beverage made from almonds. Feeling especially thrifty? Go for the a la carte bean and cheese taco with lettuce and tomato for $1.50.

You can grab a stool and eat inside along the narrow red shelf that flares out from the walls, or take your meal with you. Everything is bueno and gets served in Styrofoam to-go containers.

CUISINE	**American with a Eurasian twist**
LOCATION	**Downtown Wailuku**
HOURS	**Monday–Friday, 10:30 a.m. to 2:30 p.m.**
SEATING	**50**
PARKING	**Free parking in back**
OPENED	**2003 (originally in 1997)**
ALCOHOL	**No**
PLASTIC	**MC, V**

34

Iao Cafe
2051 Main St., Wailuku
Telephone 244-6816

Back in 1997, Dana and Michael Pastula's new Café O'Lei was a welcome addition to the Wailuku dining scene. Their first Café O'Lei, after all, was—and still is—a popular fixture in Upcountry Makawao. The Pastulas later opened a newer Café O'Lei in Lahaina, but the Wailuku eatery remained our favorite, with its no-fuss, down-home atmosphere.

Both former executive chefs, Dana and Michael built their menu around super-fresh ingredients grown by Ha'iku and Kula farmers. Recently, the Pastulas sold the Wailuku Café O'Lei to another husband-and-wife team, Claude and Carole Lucas, who renamed it the Iao Cafe and now carry on with the same good food and the same fine cooks.

The large, underdressed restaurant in Wailuku is walking distance from the courthouse and downtown businesses, so it fills up at lunch with a local crowd of County workers and shop owners in search of great food.

There are several daily specials and a soup of the day on the menu board at the Main Street entrance. We love the mahimahi plate with rice and salad greens for $6.95. The tender fish is sautéed in a lemon caper sauce and served over steamed white rice with a side of mixed vegetables.

Select from an assortment of teas served in a traditional Chinese pot for only $1. The homemade honey lemonade is a refreshing treat at $1.50.

It's a great price, and you can get it at a great place— the Iao Cafe.

CUISINE	**Cal-Mex (California-Mexican)**
LOCATION	**Dairy Road Center near Kinko's**
HOURS	**Monday–Saturday, 10:30 a.m. to 8 p.m.; Sunday, 11 a.m. to 8 p.m.**
SEATING	**43**
PARKING	**Adequate free parking at Dairy Center**
OPENED	**September 1991**
ALCOHOL	**Mexican and domestic beers, wine, wine coolers**
PLASTIC	**MC, V**
NOTES	**Daily happy hour 3 to 6 p.m.; second alcoholic beverage half-price; discounted appetizers. A portion of burrito sales goes to the Maui Humane Society.**

35

Las Piñatas of Maui
395 Dairy Rd., Kahului
Telephone 877-8707

It's a couple's last vacation day on Maui. Tomorrow they are supposed to fly back to their corporate lives in Dallas. Instead, they buy a Mexican food restaurant on Maui and decide to live happily ever after.

Steve and Lesley Hargrove did exactly that in 1995, taking over the reins (and keeping the recipes) of Las Piñatas, one of Kahului's most popular restaurants. Their menu is California-style Mexican, with lots of fresh, healthy ingredients, homemade sauces and no lard.

The hard-shell Beef Tacos Combo Plate ($6.75) is wickedly tasty. Two taco shells, filled with seasoned beef, are deep-fried and served with a sea of refried beans and rice. It's almost too large, but we manage to polish it off every time.

Then there are the Kitchen Sink Burritos, so enormous you could hide your face behind one.

We like the vegetarian ($6.75), stuffed with beans, rice, shredded lettuce and cabbage, tomatoes, sour cream, guacamole and cheese. A vegan version is also available. Like spicy? Get it smothered in a zesty green ranchero sauce for $2.10 more.

Try the specials, like chili rellenos or fresh fish tacos ($8 for the plate/$3.25 for one). You can't go wrong here. The kitchen crew is largely Hispanic, and they cook everything just right.

Las Piñatas hops at lunchtime, and it's challenging to find a table. The best time to go is around 3 p.m., just in time for happy hour. Order a cerveza and the second one is half price. The Mexican music is loud, the air-conditioning cranks and the ceiling is festooned with a kaleidoscope of piñatas. Olé!

CUISINE	**Puerto Rican**
LOCATION	**Between Hanamau Street and Wākea Avenue**
HOURS	**Monday–Friday, 7 a.m. to 2 p.m.**
SEATING	**40**
PARKING	**Free parking lot in front**
OPENED	**1984**
ALCOHOL	**No**
PLASTIC	**Cash only**

36

Mama Ding's Restaurant & Bakery
225 Alamaha St., Kahului
Telephone 877-5796

Mama Ding's is an unpretentious Puerto Rican restaurant hidden in Kahului that might go unnoticed if not for the sprawling, delightfully gaudy mural outside.

The specialty here: hot little meat turnovers stuffed with chicken or pork called empanadillas. These savory pies have a marvelous flaky, dense, golden brown crust and—watch out!—they are highly addictive. It's hard to believe they're only a buck each; $11 a dozen.

We dropped by to try the special Puerto Rican bean stew called habichuela suggested by our friend Ka'eo. For $6 you get a walloping bowlful of the hearty stew, a big scoop of rice, macaroni salad and pickled vegetables. What a deal! The habichuela has a wonderful, home-cooked flavor and is full of red beans, peppers and lean pieces of smoked ham. And it's filling. We had to take half home and eat the rest for dinner. It's not every day you can get two meals for $6.

(Funny that Ka'eo never mentioned the empanadillas. It's probably because they sell out every day and he didn't want us snatching them up!)

Owners Frank and Mary (Mama Ding) Carvalho's ancestors sailed to Maui from Puerto Rico in 1900 to work on the sugarcane plantations, bringing with them their own brand of island cooking. We're glad they passed their recipes down through the generations.

CUISINE	**Deli/bakery**
LOCATION	**Ocean side of Ka'ahumanu Avenue, on the Kahului side of Wailuku town**
HOURS	**Monday–Saturday, 6 a.m. to 4 p.m.; closed Sundays**
SEATING	**20 inside, 24 outside**
PARKING	**Plenty in parking lot**
OPENED	**December 1994**
ALCOHOL	**No**
PLASTIC	**Cash, local checks only**

37

Stillwell's Bakery & Cafe
1740 Ka'ahumanu Ave., Wailuku
Telephone 243-2243

This is the kind of place anyone might miss if it wasn't for word-of-mouth advertising. Stillwell's Bakery & Cafe occupies an unassuming spot off Ka'ahumanu Avenue that most people drive right by without noticing.

Not that it matters. The bustling bakery/cafe is packed at lunchtime with local police officers, hospital workers and throngs of other folks who work in the area and know this is *the* spot for a quick bite. Owners Roy and Louise Stillwell, who have some 60 years of hotel/restaurant experience between them, serve up an excellent selection of homemade soups, salads, sandwiches and noodles, with lunch service starting at 9:30 a.m. Sandwiches range in price from $6.50 for ham-and-cheese to $7.25 for egg salad. Bread choices include wheat, white, rye, croissant, focaccia, and nine-grain, and all are made fresh on the premises, lending a gourmet touch to the scrumptious sandwiches.

On the bakery side, the popular cream horn ($1.85) is a sinfully delicious flaky pastry stuffed with chilled vanilla custard, dunked in chocolate at one end and sprinkled with powdered sugar. Each bite melts in your mouth. The pumpkin and apple pies are the best we've had on the island. Also try the selection of freshly made cookies, brownies, rolls, seasonal hot cross buns —you name it, they probably make it.

We've considered moving to Wailuku just to be closer to Stillwell's.

CUISINE	**Noodles and local-style plate lunches**
LOCATION	**Millyard Plaza at Mill Street**
HOURS	**Daily, 9:30 a.m. to 9 p.m.**
SEATING	**80**
PARKING	**Plenty of free parking**
OPENED	**1996**
ALCOHOL	**No**
PLASTIC	**Cash and travelers checks only**
NOTES	**Dim sum served on Saturday**

38

Wei Wei BBQ 'n Noodle House
210 Imi Kala St. #201, Wailuku
Telephone 242-7928

Wei Wei is a modern version of the traditional Chinese noodle house, with booths instead of stools at the counter and a walk-up window for take-out orders. They make their own noodles for all dishes.

Folks file in at lunchtime for the house favorite, Cake Noodle ($6.95). It's a generous plate of small noodle cakes, pan-fried to a crispy brown but tender inside. The noodles are topped with bok choy, shrimp, chicken, broccoli, calamari, carrots, shiitake mushrooms, zucchini, onion, pork and green beans with a sauce that's a mixture of garlic, shoyu (soy) and oyster sauce. When the sauce mixes with the noodles—Bam! It's a wonderful fusion explosion in your mouth.

Daily plate specials are priced at $5.95 including Shoyu Spareribs and Chicken Katsu (breaded and fried) with rice and macaroni salad. Or try the Fried Garlic Chicken and Sweet-and-Sour Ribs with rice and mac salad. The mini plate includes just one scoop of rice.

The fried wontons are served a dozen in a basket, accompanied by a sweet-and-sour dipping sauce for $3.50. It reminds us of chips and salsa at Mexican restaurants.

If not everyone in your party wants a culinary adventure, there are a number of recognizable Asian dishes on the menu and American burgers, too.

One of the greatest things about this restaurant is that it's fast. Management fills the kitchen with staff to keep up with the demand. So hurry on over yourself!

CUISINE	**Vietnamese, with lots of vegetarian choices**
LOCATION	**At the corner of Main and Kaniela Streets**
HOURS	**Monday–Saturday, 10 a.m. to 9:30 p.m.; Sunday, 10 a.m. to 8:30 p.m.**
SEATING	**60, plus 22 on the lanai**
PARKING	**Free parking at the restaurant and on the street**
OPENED	**1995**
ALCOHOL	**Full bar**
PLASTIC	**V, MC**

39

A Saigon Cafe
1792 Main St., Wailuku
Telephone 243-9560

One of our favorite restaurants on Maui, A Saigon Cafe attracts everyone from corporate executives holding lunch meetings to Maui Community College students heading off-campus for dinner. Famous for her scrumptious Vietnamese cuisine, owner Jennifer Nguyen has been featured on the Food Network and in national epicurean magazines.

We are most impressed by the freshness of the menu ingredients. Jennifer grows herbs and vegetables in her gardens to incorporate in the recipes. You can taste the healthy difference in one bite of the Tofu Salad, a mix of freshly shredded cabbage, herbs and crisp bean curd, tossed with sweet-and-sour garlic dressing for $6.25. Meat lovers can substitute chicken for the tofu at the same price.

The Clay Pot is an all-in-one meal with chicken, shrimp, shiitake mushrooms, string beans, carrots and peas, sautéed in a flavorful blend of spices, then poured over steamed jasmine rice and served simmering in a covered clay pot. The flavors seep together, and when the lid is removed, an earthy aroma transfixes us. Choose mild, medium or hot spice for $7.95.

We love the list of mixed-upon-order beverages such as iced Vietnamese coffee (hot coffee served with sweetened condensed milk and poured over ice) for $1.95; fresh-squeezed lemonade with a magical mix of the perfect sweet/tart combination for $2.25; and a jasmine iced tea infused with herbs from Jennifer's garden for $1.95.

The quaint Saigon Cafe sits under the Main Street bridge in Old Wailuku Town, and can be challenging to find on your first visit. Don't give up—the food here is worth a few laps around the underpass.

CUISINE	**European, with local fresh fish**
LOCATION	**Wakea Business Center**
HOURS	**Lunch: Monday–Friday, 10:30 a.m. to 3 p.m.; dinner: Wednesday–Friday, 5 p.m. to 9 p.m.**
SEATING	**70**
PARKING	**Ample parking at dinner**
OPENED	**October 1998**
ALCOHOL	**Beer and wine; full bar**
PLASTIC	**MC, V**
NOTES	**Brigit & Bernard's catering clientele has included customers from the band members of Steely Dan to former Maui Mayor James "Kimo" Apana**

40

Brigit & Bernard's Garden Café
335 Ho'ohana St., Kahului
Telephone 877-6000

It's not very often we venture into Kahului for dinner—it's more of a lunch kind of town—but now that we know about Brigit and Bernard's Garden Café, that will change.

Brigit and Bernard Weber have refined the concrete heart of Kahului by opening their delightful restaurant at the Wakea Business Center. It's packed at lunchtime, but by dinner the pace winds down and European items like Jaegerschnitzel, Chicken Marsala and Pasta Al Funghi emerge.

We arrived at sundown and sat outside on the patio. A cold Bitburger brew elevated our spirits and our appetite. We zeroed in on the fresh mushroom appetizer featuring four types of sautéed mushrooms for $7.50.

Food of the goddesses! Next came super-fresh slices of locally caught, seared 'ahi.

For dinner, we went straight to Europe and tried the Jaegerschnitzel ($14.50). Schnitzel is thinly sliced, tender meat beaten into a thin sheet and sautéed—in this case, fabulous pork tenderloin. It was served with vegetables, herb jus and spaetzle, and flour-and-egg noodles with nutmeg that are boiled then pan-fried.

Bernard is Swiss, and his dreamy Swiss chocolate mousse ($5) melted in our mouths and vanished in seconds!

There are not many European cuisine restaurants on Maui, even fewer that are affordable. Brigit and Bernard have found their niche.

CUISINE **Chinese**

LOCATION **Maui Mall**

HOURS **Lunch: Monday–Friday, 10:30 a.m. to
2 p.m.; Saturday and Sunday, 10:30 a.m.
to 2:30 p.m.
Dinner: Sunday–Thursday, 5 p.m. to 9 p.m.;
Friday and Saturday, 5 p.m. to 9:30 p.m.**

SEATING **130**

PARKING **Free parking at Maui Mall**

OPENED **October 2000**

ALCOHOL **Beer and wine**

PLASTIC **A, MC, V**

41

Dragon Dragon
70 E. Ka'ahumanu Ave. (Maui Mall), Kahului
Telephone 893-1628

The search for a great Chinese restaurant can be a daunting task on Maui.

Although Chinese people migrated to Maui during the plantation era to work in the fields along with Japanese, Filipino, Portuguese and Hawaiians, most of them didn't remain on the Valley Isle. They ventured to Honolulu, Hawai'i's most populous city, in search of fortune, camaraderie and the big-city life they desired, leaving Maui lacking in good Chinese restaurants—until now.

Dragon Dragon opened in October 2000 at the Maui Mall, a central location where many locals live. The well-lit restaurant is clean and spartan.

We weren't going to waste this opportunity by ordering Sweet & Sour Pork or Stir-Fried Beef with Broccoli ($8.95 each), which you can find in any Chinese food restaurant in the Midwest. Instead we opted for adventure and started with Honey Walnut Prawns ($13.95), large prawns steamed then fried and tossed in a concoction of mayonnaise, sour cream, chili pepper and garlic. The walnuts were glazed with honey and served alongside. The dish was sprinkled with sesame seeds and served hot. We hadn't tasted anything so authentic since visiting Hong Kong.

Then it was on to the Live Crab (seasonally priced) with black bean sauce, "supreme sauce," ginger, green sauce and peppery salt. We paid $23 for 1-1/2 pounds. The succulent crab was our favorite.

The broad menu includes 16 rice and noodles dishes ranging from steamed rice ($1; serves one) to Yin and Yang Fried Rice ($13.95.)

Jasmine or oolong tea is served when you are seated and forks are available for those who haven't quite mastered chopsticks. Dragon Dragon also serves basic dim sum at lunchtime.

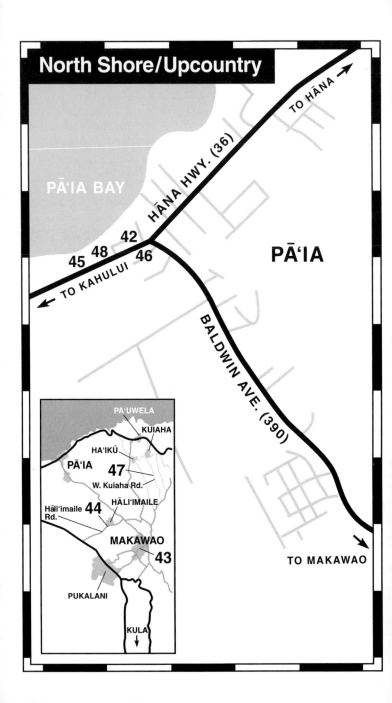

North Shore/Upcountry

PĀʻIA BAY

HĀNA HWY. (36)

TO HĀNA

42
45 48
46
TO KAHULUI

PĀʻIA

BALDWIN AVE. (390)

TO MAKAWAO

PAʻUWELA
KUIAHA
HAʻIKŪ
PĀʻIA   47
W. Kuiaha Rd.
Hāliʻimaile   44
Rd.
HĀLIʻIMAILE
MAKAWAO   43
PUKALANI

KULA

North Shore/Upcountry Restaurants
(Hāliʻimaile, Kula, Makawao, Pāʻia)

Breakfast
42. Charley's Restaurant and Saloon

Lunch
43. Casanova Italian Restaurant & Deli
44. Haliʻimaile General Store
45. Milagros
46. Paia Fishmarket
47. Pauwela Cafe and Bakery

Dinner
48. Jacques North Shore

CUISINE	**American upscale saloon**
LOCATION	**On the Hāna side of Pāʻia**
HOURS	**Breakfast: Monday–Saturday, 7 a.m. to 1 p.m.; Sunday, 7 a.m. to 2:30 p.m. Lunch: daily, 11:30 a.m. to 2:30 p.m. Dinner: nightly, 5 p.m. to 10 p.m. Late dinner menu (Woofer Menu): 10 p.m. to 2:30 a.m.**
SEATING	**185**
PARKING	**Ample free parking at restaurant**
OPENED	**July 1967**
ALCOHOL	**Full bar**
PLASTIC	**A, D, DC, MC, V**
NOTES	**Daily drink specials; evening live entertainment in the saloon**

Charley's Restaurant and Saloon
142 Hāna Hwy., Pāʻia
Telephone 579-9453

Opened in 1969, Charley's is the "old dog" of Pāʻia, literally. The owners named their restaurant and saloon after their Great Dane, Charley, and pictures throughout the saloon bear testimony to his genteel character. The restaurant section of the establishment is open for breakfast, lunch and dinner, but it was its world-famous morning meal that was voted "Best Breakfast on Maui."

We like to create our own gut-busting omelet with three ingredients for $8.50 (additional items at $1.25 each). Ingredients include feta cheese, smoked salmon, meats, vegetables, peppers, chilies and salsas. All omelets are served with a choice of home fries, rice or sliced tomato, and a choice of toast or English muffin.

From the griddle, try a cinnamon buckwheat pancake, so big it falls off the plate. It's $3.50,

but if you're really adventurous, you'll try the surfer's stack (two) for $4.75. Island sweetbread French toast is $7.50—three pieces of thick sweetbread prepared *zee* French way. Add another island twist with yummy coconut syrup.

The daily specials menu included a Cajun ʻahi (yellowfin tuna) Eggs Benedict (prepared with ono on the regular menu, it's the best-seller) with fresh Hollandaise sauce and a choice of rice, sliced tomatoes or seasoned home fries ($10.50). Superb!

Following breakfast, head out to Hoʻokipa Beach Park, 10 minutes east on Hāna Highway, and check out the sailboarding mecca that's home to the world windsurfing championships. On a less windy day, surfers will paddle out for a ride. But stay on shore unless you've already had rip-roaring wave experience yourself.

CUISINE	**American**
LOCATION	**Corner of Makawao and Baldwin Avenues**
WEB	**www.casanovamaui.com**
HOURS	**Deli: 8 a.m. to 6 p.m.** **Restaurant: lunch, 11:30 a.m. to 2 p.m.;** **dinner, 5:30 to 9:30 p.m.; live entertain-** **ment until 2 a.m. four nights a week**
SEATING	**50**
PARKING	**20 stalls next to the restaurant and along** **the street**
OPENED	**1986**
ALCOHOL	**No**
PLASTIC	**CB, D, DC, MC, V**
NOTES	**Breakfast served until 11:30 a.m.; lunch** **menu served all day**

43

Casanova Italian Restaurant and Deli

1188 Makawao Ave., Makawao
Telephone 572-0220

Locals know that Casanova Deli is the original incarnation of what is now Upcountry Maui's number-one dinner/dance spot—Casanova Italian Restaurant. For more than 15 years, Casanova Deli has served breakfast and lunch at the crossroads of Makawao and Baldwin Avenues.

The leisurely lifestyle of Makawao attracts a free-spirited crowd that makes Casanova Deli a regular stop. During our visit, we ran into Avi Kiriaty, one of Maui's preeminent fine artists, whose paintings of everyday island life depict a colorful world.

He grabbed a coffee and, in typical artist fashion, began pointing out the deli's original hardwood floors, aluminum roof and koa wood bar tops, reminiscing about the history of the place.

Breakfast is served until 11:30 a.m. daily, since many folks are slow to rise after dancing the night away next door.

The Scrambled Croissant is our favorite at $3.50. It's two scrambled eggs served on a buttery, flaky croissant made in the cafe kitchen. Add cheese for 50 cents, or bacon for $1 more, and you have a hearty meal. They'll also substitute egg whites at no extra charge.

The more, the better when it comes to good food, we always say. So we ordered the Lox and Bagel for $6.25. A thinly sliced serving of fresh salmon, cream cheese, chopped green onions, capers, tomatoes and sprouts, it was wonderfully satisfying.

Assorted pastries, quiches and lunch items are displayed in the deli case for your choosing. Espresso ($1.50 single, $2.25 double) and fruit smoothies ($3) are made to order at the counter, and folks eat in on koa wood belly bars or sit outside along the lanai bar facing the avenue.

CUISINE	**Eclectic American with Asian overtones**
LOCATION	**A mile-and-a-half off Highway 37 on Hāliʻimaile Road**
HOURS	**Lunch: Monday–Friday, 11 a.m to 2:30 p.m.** **Dinner: Nightly, 5:30 p.m. to 9:30 p.m.**
SEATING	**130**
PARKING	**Plenty of free parking available**
OPENED	**October 1988**
ALCOHOL	**Full bar, wine list**
PLASTIC	**A, D, DC, JCB, MC, V**
NOTES	**Bev and her husband, Joe, also own Joe's Bar & Grill in Wailea.**

44

Hali'imaile General Store
900 Hāli'imaile Rd., Hāli'imaile
Telephone 572-2666

Eating lunch at Hali'imaile General Store is like having a gourmet picnic catered for you in the middle of a pineapple plantation.

The refurbished general store is surrounded by 1,000 acres of Maui's famed fruit in Hāli'imaile, which is "Upcountry" without going all the way up. Owner-chef Beverly Gannon, a founding member of the Hawai'i Regional Cuisine movement, elevates classic lunch items into their own stratosphere.

A chicken club, for example, becomes the Hali'imaile Oven-Roasted Chicken Club, with caramelized Maui onions, brie and bacon on sourdough ($9). A quesadilla here is filled with smoked Gouda, Szechuan salmon and scallions and topped with chipotle crème and guacamole ($10). And Bev's Chinese Chicken Salad ($12) is anything but ordinary, with its baby corn, raisins, water chestnuts and crispy wontons.

If you don't mind spending a bit more, try the catch of the day. Beverly has a flair for fresh fish; her 'Ahi Nicoise ($14) is also excellent.

Bev shows her southern roots with dishes like Rock Shrimp and Crab Cakes ($12), Infamous Baby Back Ribs ($12) and her famous Crab Pizza ($8).

We're glad chef Bev serves lunch at her esteemed restaurant. It's less expensive than the dinner menu and offers a welcome retreat from the resort scene.

CUISINE	**Southwestern with an island flair**
LOCATION	**On the corner of Hāna Highway and Baldwin Avenue**
HOURS	**Daily, 8 a.m. to 10 p.m.; bar closes at 11 p.m.**
SEATING	**28 outside, 36 inside**
PARKING	**Free parking lot in back off Hāna Highway**
OPENED	**April 1995**
ALCOHOL	**Full bar, draft beer**
PLASTIC	**A, JCB, MC, V**
NOTES	**Keiki menu; also daily drink specials from 3 to 6 p.m.**

45

Milagros
3 Baldwin Ave., Pā'ia
Telephone 579-8755

Size matters for some people, and Milagros caters to a hearty appetite.

Milagros (Spanish for miracles) is a miraculous little joint located at the main crossroads in Pā'ia. We were amazed that we couldn't find anything on the menu over $9.50. And just about everything is made from scratch, even the tortilla chips.

We heard the fish tacos are Milagros' pièce de résistance, so we tried them with 'ahi ($8.25 for two tacos, plus homemade black beans and Spanish rice) and found them to be light and tasty, with a smoky sweet hint of chipotle pepper. A towering mound of black bean nachos ($6.95) and a fresh baby spinach salad ($6.95) with blue cheese crumbles and papaya seed were both delectable.

We spent a good part of a Sunday afternoon people-watching from our table outside, sipping Paia Punch, a rum drink made with pineapple and orange juice ($4.75). A nonstop parade of surfers, shoppers and dread-locked Deadheads kept us quite entertained. We contemplated the tequila menu, which features an array of premium shots for $6, but decided against it. Beer aficionados will appreciate the nice selection of microbrews on tap.

If you like dessert, save room for the Brownie Sandwich. It's available only at night, for $6. (See "Sweet Endings" on page 114.)

CUISINE	**Fresh fish**
LOCATION	**At the intersection of Hāna Highway and Baldwin Avenue, across from Milagros**
HOURS	**Daily, 11 a.m. to 9:30 p.m.**
SEATING	**56**
PARKING	**Free parking lot up Baldwin on the left; nearby stalls**
OPENED	**August 1989**
ALCOHOL	**Beer & wine**
PLASTIC	**D, DC, MC, V**
NOTES	**Check out the fresh fish specials on the signboard at the door.**

46

Paia Fishmarket
100 Hāna Hwy., Pā'ia
Telephone 579-8030

We've been coming to Paia Fishmarket for years, but we'd always ordered the same two things: The grilled ono fish sandwich and the fish tacos.

On our latest trip, Yuri Soledad, a 25-year-old Brazilian surfer who worked his way from dishwasher to partner, persuaded us to buck the trend. We could have our fish tacos, but his way: Cajun-style 'ahi tacos.

Sold. But first we tried the exquisite blackened 'ahi sashimi ($11.95), which comes sliced in bright red squares framed by Cajun spice and slices of pink, peppery ginger. The Cajun fish taco ($4, a la carte) arrived in corn tortillas with a side of home-made dill tartar sauce—love at first bite. A sea of seafood pasta was next: Creamy waves of linguine tossed with fresh fish, scallops and large shrimp, and topped with fresh Parmesan and capers. It's large enough for two.

Paia Fishmarket is an ideal place to try fresh Hawaiian fish without spending a fortune; it offers several different fish specialties a day in a variety of preparations. The place has surf-shack soul, with woven lau hala wall mats, surf art and a catchy "fish print" of a real octopus. Seating is on long, wide picnic tables, each accommodating up to eight people.

Do try that ono sandwich ($6.50). Ono is a type of mackerel known for its firm, white flesh. Here it's grilled and served on a fresh bun with coleslaw, tomato, cheese and scrumptious home-made tartar sauce. As the locals say, "Broke da mout'!"

CUISINE	**Eclectic American**
LOCATION	**Pauwela Cannery**
HOURS	**Monday–Saturday, 7 a.m. to 3 p.m.; Sunday, 8 a.m. to 2 p.m.**
SEATING	**15 inside, 20 outside**
PARKING	**Plenty of free parking along the Cannery and the street**
OPENED	**June 1994**
ALCOHOL	**No**
PLASTIC	**Cash and travelers checks only**
NOTES	**Becky does all the baking.**

47

Pauwela Cafe and Bakery
375 West Kuiaha Rd., Ha'ikū
Telephone 575-9242

We read about Pauwela Cafe and Bakery in a column by another food writer and decided we had to make the long drive from Lahaina to Ha'ikū to see if it was *all that*.

The cheery decor and wholesome food is definitely worth the fuel. Plus it's on the way to Hāna, so it's a perfect place to grab food for the trip. We gobbled down the famed warm Kalua Turkey Sandwich ($6.25). It's a colossal creation, stuffed with shredded, smoked kālua turkey, jack cheese and tasty bits of mild green chilies. The dressing is homemade cilantro pesto and mayonnaise, spread on homemade French bread with a side of green salad.

As we sipped a cup of frothy cappuccino ($2.25), we decided this just might be the best sandwich on Maui.

Becky Speere, who owns the cafe with her husband, arrives at 3:30 a.m. to bake her own breads, pastries and muffins. All sauces and dressings are homemade, too, and it shows.

Breakfast favorites include Pain Perdu, a French bread dipped in rich orange custard and baked golden brown with real maple syrup for $4.75, and Eggs Chilaquile ($5.75), a Mexican classic layered with beans, tortillas, chilies and cheese, topped with a light egg custard and baked.

The cafe is in the historic Pauwela Cannery, a pineapple-cannery-turned-artists'-colony teeming with surfboard shapers, graphic designers, woodworkers and other artisans.

CUISINE	**Seafood/sushi**
LOCATION	**Right on Pā'ia's main drag**
HOURS	**Daily, 5 to 10 p.m.; bar open as late as 1:30 a.m.**
SEATING	**170**
PARKING	**Free parking in gravel lot in back; limited parking along Hāna Highway**
OPENED	**1998**
ALCOHOL	**Full bar**
PLASTIC	**A, D, DC, MC, V**
NOTES	**No sushi on Sunday and Monday; no reservations needed**

48

Jacques North Shore
120 Hana Hwy., Pāʻia
Telephone 579-8844

Jacques is the north shore's hippest spot, with a young energy vibrating from its eclectic outdoor restaurant and sushi bar. Toned and tanned windsurfers and surfers gather here with other north shore residents to meet after a day in the waves.

Jacques Pauvert is chef/owner, and his recipe for success includes hiring the island's most gorgeous hostesses and dressing them in "barely there" clothing for a wonderful display of eye candy. We felt the groove and donned our funky island best for the occasion.

Some compare Jacques' fish entrees with Mama's Fish House down the road, without the higher prices. And others find it surprising that the food is so good, given the great deals.

We ordered the Stuffed Salmon with Crab and Gorgonzola Cheese wrapped in nori ($24.95), resembling a grand sushi roll. It's served with teriyaki sauce, and the rich cheese flavor makes this dish pop. Wow! It deserves a medal for originality.

Our favorite preparation is the North Shore Pumpkin Fish ($14.95)—fresh fish, bananas and oranges served with a ginger pumpkin sauce and miso butter. All fish entrees are served with seasonal vegetables and rice.

There are plenty of health-minded people in the area, so Jacques peppers the large menu with a selection of vegan and vegetarian entrees. And the funky sushi bar tucked inside gives you a reason to visit Jacques again.

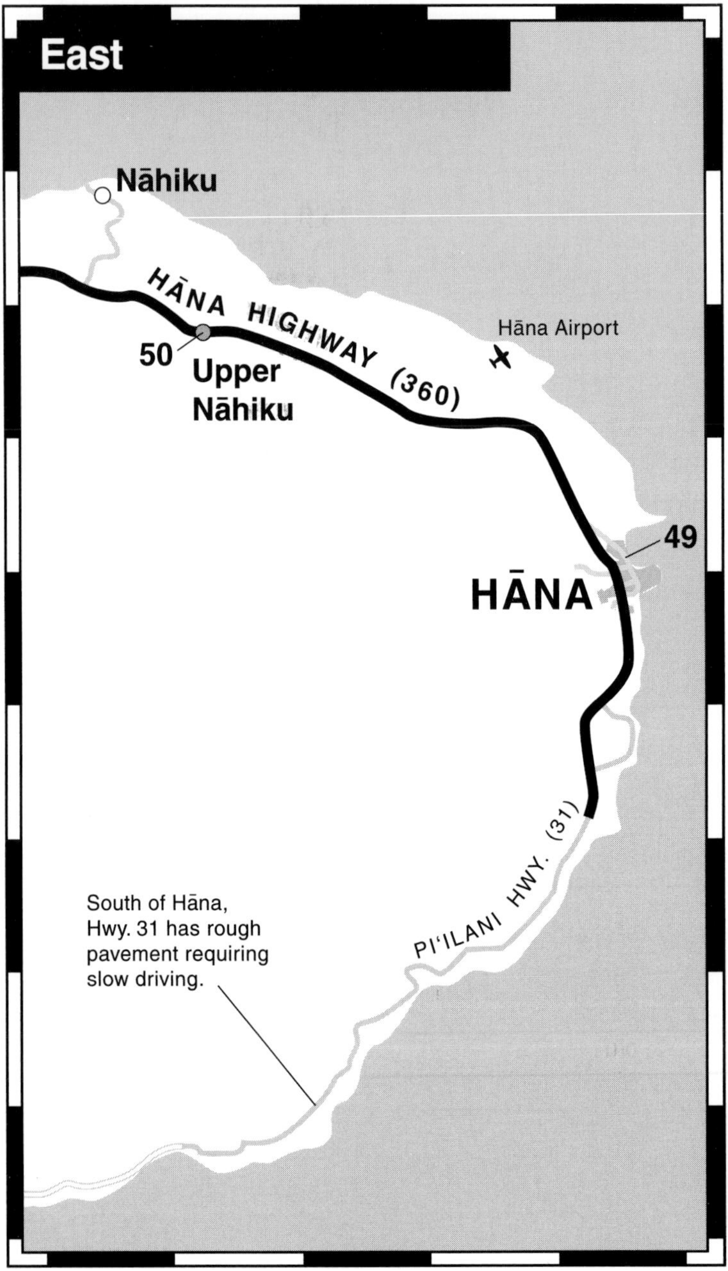

East

Nāhiku

HĀNA HIGHWAY (360)

Hāna Airport

50 Upper Nāhiku

49

HĀNA

PI'ILANI HWY. (31)

South of Hāna, Hwy. 31 has rough pavement requiring slow driving.

East Maui Restaurants
(Hāna, Nāhiku)

Lunch
49. Tutu's
50. Up in Smoke

CUISINE	Casual American/local plate lunch
LOCATION	At Hāna Bay in the Helene Hall Community Building
HOURS	Daily, 8 a.m. to 4 p.m.; grill closes at 3:45 p.m.
SEATING	20 outside Tutu's, picnic tables across the road at Hāna Bay Park
PARKING	Free parking in nearby stalls
OPENED	1972
ALCOHOL	No
PLASTIC	Cash and travelers checks only
NOTES	Daily plate lunch specials

Tutu's
At Hāna Bay
Telephone 248-8224

I f you've been to Hāna, you've probably seen Tutu's burger stand at Hāna Bay. If you're headed to Hāna without your own lunch, you'll want to know where Tutu's is.

Hāna, although rich in scenery and Hawaiian history, doesn't have much to offer in the restaurant department. Tutu's is a welcome oasis for hungry, road-weary travelers and Hāna locals alike.

There are some tasty surprises on the menu, too. For instance, the Taro Burger is the Hawaiian version of a veggie burger, a grilled Technicolor patty of taro (the perennial Polynesian staple), brown rice, Moloka'i sweet potato, carrots, sunflower seeds, garlic and other healthy ingredients for $5.25. The burger, with its vivid purple potato chunks and shreds of orange carrot, is flavorful and moist, and fun to examine after every bite.

Our companion opted for Tutu's Burger, a basic hamburger served on a grilled bun with lettuce and tomato for $4.75. We drank fountain Cokes at $1.50 each.

There are several large tables at the community center where Tutu's is located, but most people carry lunch across the road to the bayside picnic tables at Hāna Bay Park. It's a laid-back, scenic park and a good place to absorb the local flavor, or to plan the next step of your Hāna adventure.

CUISINE	**Roadside barbecue**
LOCATION	**Nāhiku, on the way to Hāna, next to the Nahiku Cafe**
HOURS	**Friday–Wednesday, 10 a.m. to 5 p.m.; closed Thursday**
SEATING	**10, additional seating at Nahiku Cafe**
PARKING	**Plenty of parking off Hāna Highway**
OPENED	**July 1998**
ALCOHOL	**No**
PLASTIC	**Cash only**

50

Up in Smoke
Hāna Hwy. between mile markers 28 & 29, Nāhiku
No telephone

The only commercial food options for folks heading to Hāna used to be in Pā'ia. That's changed. Along with emerging fruit stands and coffee pit stops, there is now a bona fide, mouth-watering road-side barbecue operating next to the Nahiku Cafe.

With its Hawaiian-style lanai, the esoteric establishment could easily be mistaken for someone's residential barbecue, but the rental cars pulled off to the side of the road hint at something special.

The young husband-and-wife owners, Linda and Carl Ebrus, buy fresh fish daily from local fishermen. They grill the catch of the day, local corn on the cob (in season) and breadfruit wrapped in banana leaf on a kiawe wood-burning grill.

The five-ounce fish filet is threaded on a bamboo skewer much like a kabob, and the "fish sticks" sell for $4. But it's not really a barbecue unless you have ribs on the grill, right? On Saturdays, the Ebruses slow-cook slabs of hearty baby back pork ribs and sell three of them for $4, or six for $7.

The kālua (smoked) pork sandwich is piled high on a sesame seed bun for $4. And organic, free-range, hard-boiled chicken eggs sell for 50 cents each.

You'll have to get your beverages next door at the Nahiku Cafe, which sells coffee, espresso, smoothies, sodas and juices. The cafe also has enormous chocolate chip and peanut butter cookies in a basket next to the register. Grab one for the road.

Linda and Carl have been in business for five years, so they've built up a faithful repeat clientele. They enjoy the rural lifestyle and have combined this with their passion for cooking to create one of the best pit stops in East Maui.

Sweet Endings

A Baker's Dozen of Maui's Best, Least Expensive Desserts

JESSICA'S PICKS

Milagros Brownie Sandwich, $6 *(A chocolate macadamia nut brownie with hot chocolate sauce, topped with vanilla ice cream, caramelized bananas and whipped cream.)* 3 Baldwin Ave., Pā'ia

BJ's Chicago Pizzeria Pizookie, $4.95 *(A huge chocolate chip cookie baked and served piping hot in its own mini-pizza pan, with a whopping scoop of vanilla ice cream.)* 730 Front St., Lahaina

Stillwell's Bakery and Cafe Cream Horn, $1.85 *(Pastry of chilled vanilla custard cream dipped in chocolate.)* 1740 Ka'ahumanu Ave., Wailuku

Tutu's Roselani brand Haupia Ice Cream, $2.40 a scoop *(Haupia is a Hawaiian pudding of coconut milk, sugar and arrowroot, served chilled in squares at lū'au. It makes superlative ice cream.)* Helene Hall Community Building, Hāna

Brigit & Bernard's Garden Café Swiss Chocolate Mousse, $5 *(Bernard is Swiss and he knows his mousse!)* 335 Ho'ohana St., Kahului

Pita Paradise Baklava Ice Cream Cake, $5.95 a slice *(Vanilla ice cream cake with baklava layers. Baklava is a traditional Middle Eastern sweet pastry made with buttered phyllo dough layered with nuts, honey and cinnamon.)*
1913 S. Kīhei Rd., Kīhei

Pauwela Café and Bakery Fresh Maui Pineapple Upside-Down Cake, $3 a slice *(The classic, with fresh Maui pineapple.)* 375 W. Kuiaha Rd., Ha'ikū

YVONNE'S PICKS

Marco's Grill & Deli Lovin' Spoonful Fudge Cake, $5.95 *(Extravagantly moist fudge chocolate layer cake served warm with whipped cream and chocolate syrup.)* 444 Hāna Hwy., Kahului

Komoda Store & Bakery Cream Puff, $1.05 *(Former Maui County Mayor James "Kimo" Apana's favorite!)* 3674 Baldwin Ave., Makawao

Grandma's Coffee House Homemade Carrot Cake, $3.25 a slice *(Another great reason to drive to Hāna the back way.)* 153 Kula Hwy., Kēōkea

Joe's Bar & Grill Chocolate Bread Pudding, $6 *(The classic dessert made famous by Joe's daughter, pastry chef Teresa "Cheech" Gannon Shurilla.)* 131 Wailea Ike Pl., Wailea

Tom's Mini Mart The best shave ice on the island, $1.75 for three flavors *(Harry Eagar of* The Maui News *stops here often. Real shave ice shouldn't taste like a snow cone; the ice is shaved even finer and served with local flavors such as haupia and green tea.)* 372 Waiehu Beach Rd., Waiehu

Tasaka Guri-Guri Fantastic sherbet, $1.40 to $1.70 a scoop *(So delicious that locals from the other islands take it home for gifts.)* Maui Mall, Kahului

Glossary

'ahi	yellowfin tuna
bok choy	Chinese cabbage
cerveza	beer, ale
chow fun	silky rice noodles with stir-fried vegetables
cone sushi	sweet vinegar-flavored rice wrapped in fried tofu
haupia	Hawaiian coconut pudding
kālua pork	smoked, shredded pork
keiki	child
kiawe	algaroba tree, mesquite
kim chee	Korean spicy, salty pickled cabbage
laulau	meat or vegetables wrapped in ti and taro leaves and steamed
lomilomi salmon	chopped salmon with diced tomatoes and onions
lū'au	Hawaiian feast
lumpia	Filipino spring roll

mahimahi	dolphinfish, dorado
miso	fermented soybean paste
musubi	rice ball
nori	seaweed
ono	mackerel
'ono	delicious
poi	taro paste
pūpū	hors d'oeuvres
saimin	thin noodles in broth
sake	rice wine
sashimi	raw fish
shoyu	soy sauce
taro	Polynesian staple plant
tempura	shrimp or vegetables battered and deep-fried
wonton	Chinese dumplings filled with pork, shrimp and vegetables

About the Authors

A specialist in travel and hospitality communications for more than a decade, longtime Maui resident **Yvonne Biegel** has represented three of Hawai'i's AAA Five Diamond luxury resort properties—as Regional Director of Public Relations for Four Seasons Resorts Hawaii —Maui and Hualalai and as Director of Public Relations for The Ritz-Carlton, Kapalua. In 2000, she launched a successful public relations and marketing agency, Biegel Communications, with an impressive client list that includes some of Maui's top chefs. A recipient of *Pacific Business News'* "Forty Under 40" award in 2001, Yvonne continues to work with local chefs and businesses to promote their talents and products.

Jessica Ferracane grew up in Hawai'i and was a Maui-based journalist for a decade before changing lanes—and islands—to pursue a career in public relations. She is currently employed as Director of Public Relations at The Fairmont Orchid, Hawai'i, on the Kohala Coast of Hawai'i's Big Island, where she indulges in delicious cuisine every chance she gets.

Index

A Saigon Cafe 86
Alexander's Fish, Chicken and Chips .54
Aloha Mixed Plate 20
Azeka's Ribs & Snack Shop 44
Bale French Sandwich & Bakery 22
Bentos & Banquets 72
Brigit & Bernard's Garden Café 88
Casanova 96
Castaway Cafe 6
Charley's Restaurant and Saloon . . .94
Compadres Bar & Grill 8
Da Kitchen Express 46
DeanO's Maui Pizza Café 56
Dragon Dragon 90
Fiesta Time 74
Gaby's Pizzeria & Deli 28
Hali'imaile General Store 98
Honokowai Okazuya & Deli 24
Honolua Store 26
Iao Cafe 76
Jacques North Shore 106
Jonny's Burger Joint 30
Joy's Place 48
Kihei Caffe 40
Lahaina Coolers 32

Lahaina Sushiya 10
Las Piñatas of Maui 78
Mama Ding's 80
Maui Coffee Roasters 64
Maui Tacos 50
Milagros 100
Moose McGillycuddy's 12
Paia Fishmarket 102
Pauwela Cafe and Bakery 104
Peggy Sue's 58
Penne Pasta Cafe 34
Pita Paradise 52
Sam Sato's 66
Soup Nutz and Java Jazz 14
Stella Blues Cafe 42
Stillwell's Bakery 82
Sunrise Cafe 16
Sushi Go! 60
Take Home Maui 18
Tasty Crust 68
Thai Chef Restaurant 36
The Dunes Restaurant 70
Tutu's .110
Up in Smoke 112
Wei Wei BBQ 84

Order More Hawai‘i Dining Guides
from Watermark Publishing

Watermark Publishing
1000 Bishop Street, Suite 806
Honolulu, Hawaii 96813

Toll-free 1-866-900-BOOK
sales@bookshawaii.net

Name _____ Phone _____

Address _____

City _____ State _____ Zip _____

TITLE	PRICE	QTY.	
50 Thrifty Maui Restaurants	$6.95 x _____	=	$ _____
The Puka Guide	$8.95 x _____	=	$ _____
The Okazu Guide	$8.95 x _____	=	$ _____
The Omiyage Guide	$8.95 x _____	=	$ _____
Shipping & handling (USPS Priority Mail)*			$ _____
TOTAL ORDER			$ _____

☐ Check enclosed, payable to Watermark Publishing

☐ Charge my credit card   ☐ Visa   ☐ MC   ☐ Amex

                 ☐ Discover   ☐ Diner's   ☐ Carte Blanche

Card no. _____ Exp. date _____

Signature Required _____

* $2 each up to 10 copies, $1 each 11-50 copies, call for more than 50